Thinking Skills for Tests

Upper Elementary

Thinking Skills for Tests products available in print or eBook form.

Early Learning (PreK-2)
Upper Elementary (Grades 3-5)

Written by
Robin MacFarlane, Ph.D.

Edited by
Patricia Gray

Graphic Design by
Scott Slyter

© 2013
THE CRITICAL THINKING CO.™
www.CriticalThinking.com
Phone: 800-458-4849 • Fax: 541-756-1758
1991 Sherman Ave., Suite 200 • North Bend • OR 97459
ISBN 978-1-60144-579-7

Reproduction of This Copyrighted Material
The intellectual material in this product is the copyrighted property of The Critical Thinking Co.™ The individual or entity who initially purchased this product from The Critical Thinking Co.™ or one of its authorized resellers is licensed to reproduce (print or duplicate on paper) each page of this product for use within one home or one classroom. Our copyright and this limited reproduction permission (user) agreement strictly prohibit the sale of any of the copyrighted material in this product. Any reproduction beyond these expressed limits is strictly prohibited without the written permission of The Critical Thinking Co.™ Please visit http://www.criticalthinking.com/copyright for more information. The Critical Thinking Co.™ retains full intellectual property rights on all its products (eBooks, books, and software).
Printed in China by Hangzhou Hua'an Printing Co., Ltd. (Jan. 2016)

TABLE OF CONTENTS

© 2013 The Critical Thinking Co.™ • www.CriticalThinking.com • 800-458-4849

INTRODUCTION

*Thinking Skills for Tests: Upper Elementary*** teaches test-taking skills that will help students in Grades 3-5 to perform their best on standardized tests. Usually students prepare for standardized tests by taking practice tests, but without explicit instruction in test-taking skills, time spent taking practice tests can be counterproductive. Practice tests alone may only reinforce ineffective test-taking habits. *Thinking Skills for Tests* develops effective but often overlooked ways to think about the common parts of almost all standardized tests.

Students can learn to:
- consider each answer choice in a way that will increase the likelihood of giving a correct answer rather than an impressionistic wrong answer that might *seem* correct.

- expect that they will not understand every detail of what they read in reading comprehension passages.

- understand the main idea of a passage, regardless of whether or not they understand many of the details, and effectively answer questions based on what they *do* know.

- preview questions in a way that research shows can improve test performance.

- give short, written answers to questions that will be clear to any reader, even one who is unfamiliar with test content, which will increase the quality of written answers.

- make inferences about what they read on a test or in a passage.

- estimate answers to math problems in order to check their work and also know when it's appropriate to use estimation to give answers to test questions.

- translate different types of mathematical word problems into math problems that lead to the correct solution. This process involves discerning those parts of word problems that are necessary for finding the solution, using the correct math operation, and checking answers.

- appreciate the patterns involved in both visual and numerical test questions.

**Thinking Skills for Tests: Upper Elementary* was prepared following ethical guidelines provided by the National Council on Measurement in Education. The content bears no strong resemblance to any actual assessment or specific items from any assessment. Students who practice with *Thinking Skills for Tests* may perform better on standardized tests than they would without this practice, but their test scores will not rise beyond their actual ability levels.

Thinking Skills for Tests is a systematic method of practicing critical thinking in a test-taking format that can build a student's confidence and skill knowledge. It is not designed to be scored or used as an indicator of academic or test performance.

Level of Difficulty

Thinking Skills for Tests: Upper Elementary is appropriate for students who have, at least, completed most of a 3rd grade curriculum. Test-taking skills are presented and practiced. Optional material is available for advanced students who would like to practice their test-taking skills with more difficult test questions after completing all the skills. Advanced students should not skip ahead to the advanced sections because this will prevent them from learning the test-taking skills.

Work in the Order That the Chapters Are Presented

It is recommended that students work through the chapters in the order in which they are presented because the material is cumulative. Basic test-taking skills learned in the first chapter, *Vocabulary*, are used in almost all of the subsequent sections. Also, reading comprehension skills are applied to mathematical word problems. The most important sections that contain material used in subsequent sections are *Vocabulary, Answer Multiple Choice Questions, Give Written Answers,* and *Solve Complicated Word Problems*. When students learn in the order in which the material is presented, they gain the full benefit of using this book.

Acknowledgement
Many thanks to Claire Tempelman for sharing her editorial skill and guidance.

© 2013 The Critical Thinking Co.™ • www.CriticalThinking.com • 800-458-4849

I. Vocabulary

What does the word vocabulary mean?

Your vocabulary is how you use all the words you know. At this time in your life, your vocabulary is growing very quickly. What makes your vocabulary grow? Reading!

Sometimes when you read for fun, you see words you do not know. You figure out what those words mean by reading the rest of the sentence or paragraph and deciding on a meaning that fits the word. The other words in the sentence give you clues about the meaning of the word you don't know. You probably don't even know that's what you're doing when you read! As you figure out the meaning of words, you do a lot of thinking without even being aware of it.

When you are tested on vocabulary, you may run into words you do not know. You can look for clues in the sentence just like you do when you read for fun. However, when you are taking a test you need to be more careful and aware of what you are doing. The following are steps that will help you think carefully about vocabulary words on a test.

Step 1: Think about what the word means *before* you look at the answer choices.

Let's pretend that you are reading a book and read this sentence:

It was <u>gelid</u> on the morning of the first day of winter, and frost was on the window.

You know a lot of words, but you probably have never heard the word <u>gelid</u>. To figure out what <u>gelid</u> means, you will use clues. Here are two clues:
- It was the first day of winter.
- There was frost on the window.

Write what you think <u>gelid</u> probably means. _____

When you read for fun, you learn the meaning of new words by looking for clues in the rest of the sentence. On a test, you do the same thing! Also, a test usually gives you extra help because of answer choices!

It was <u>gelid</u> on the morning of the first day of winter, and frost was on the window.
- a. sunny
- b. icy
- c. night
- d. hot

Have you figured out the answer? You probably have a good idea about which answer is correct. In order to make sure that you are thinking carefully about each answer choice, move on to Step 2: Try each answer choice in the sentence.

© 2013 The Critical Thinking Co.™ • www.CriticalThinking.com • 800-458-4849

Step 2: Try each answer choice in the sentence.

On a test, you must look at each answer choice, <u>even if you think you know the right answer</u>. Here you will see how you can think carefully about each answer choice by trying each one in the sentence.

Read each sentence below. Then mark "yes" if the underlined word makes sense in the new sentence or "no" if it does not make sense.

1. It was <u>sunny</u> on the morning of the first day of winter, and frost was on the window.
    ○ yes   ○ no   (*This makes sense. There are cold, sunny mornings in winter.*)

2. It was <u>icy</u> on the morning of the first day of winter, and frost was on the window.
    ○ yes   ○ no   (*This makes sense. There are icy mornings in winter.*)

3. It was <u>night</u> on the morning of the first day of winter, and frost was on the window.
    ○ yes   ○ no   (*This does not make sense. It is never night in the morning!*)

4. It was <u>hot</u> on the morning of the first day of winter, and frost was on the window.
    ○ yes   ○ no   (*This does not make sense. It cannot be hot if there is frost on the window.*)

Step 3: Cross out answer choices that do not make sense.

Now you know that there are two answers that don't make sense. The answer is not "night" or "hot," so cross them out.

a. sunny
b. icy
c. ~~night~~
d. ~~hot~~

You are left with two answers that could be correct. "Sunny" makes sense, and "icy" makes sense.

So what do you do when you have two or more answers that could be correct? You choose the best answer, which is Step 4.

© 2013 The Critical Thinking Co.™ • www.CriticalThinking.com • 800-458-4849

Step 4: Choose the best answer.

If you're sure which answer is best, even though other answers might be correct, then choose that answer.

"I'm sure of the best answer! So it's easy. I choose the answer that I'm sure is best!"

If you are <u>not</u> sure which answer is best, there are two things that can help you:

"I'm not sure! So I have to look at what I wrote <u>before</u> I saw the answer choices. If that doesn't help, I'll take a guess."

a. Look at the answer you wrote *before* you saw the answer choices.

When you read the sentence for the first time, you had a feeling about what the word <u>gelid</u> meant. You even wrote that word down. So, you should choose the answer that is closest to the word that you wrote down. <u>Usually the first feeling you have about what a word means is a very important thing to notice, because a lot of times, you are correct.</u>

b. Take a guess!

There are many, many times you won't know the right answer on a test. It is okay to guess! Also, remember, you have already crossed out answers that don't make sense. So you have fewer answers to choose from. If you guess, you will be making a very good guess.

Remember when you wrote down what you thought <u>gelid</u> meant? You probably wrote something like "cold," "chilly," or "snowy," which are all similar to "icy."

a. sunny
b. icy
c. ~~night~~
d. ~~hot~~

Even though "sunny" could be correct, "icy" is the best answer.

© 2013 The Critical Thinking Co.™ • www.CriticalThinking.com • 800-458-4849

Guided Practice

You just learned these four steps that will help you find the correct answers to questions about your vocabulary:

Step 1: Think about what the word means before you look at the answer choices.
Step 2: Try each answer choice in the sentence.
Step 3: Cross out answer choices that do not make sense.
Step 4: Choose the best answer.

Now you will practice each of the steps in the next exercises. These exercises guide you through each step. After you practice, you will feel more confident when you answer vocabulary questions.

Exercise 1

Step 1: Think about what the word means *before* you look at the answer choices.

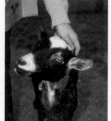 After you touch animals in a petting zoo, it is important to <u>sanitize</u> your hands.

I think <u>sanitize</u> means _____.

Are you having trouble thinking of what the word might mean? Just take a guess!

Clue: After you touch animals, your hands are dirty.

Step 2: Try each answer choice in the sentence.

After you touch animals in a petting zoo, it is important to <u>sanitize</u> your hands.
   a. clap
   b. wash
   c. smell
   d. raise

Don't choose your answer yet — go through all the steps first!

Which of the following sentences make sense?
1. After you touch animals in a petting zoo, it is important to <u>clap</u> your hands.
    ○ yes   ○ no

2. After you touch animals in a petting zoo, it is important to <u>wash</u> your hands.
    ○ yes   ○ no

3. After you touch animals in a petting zoo, it is important to <u>smell</u> your hands.
    ○ yes   ○ no

4. After you touch animals in a petting zoo, it is important to <u>raise</u> your hands.
    ○ yes   ○ no

© 2013 The Critical Thinking Co.™ • www.CriticalThinking.com • 800-458-4849

Step 3: Cross out answer choices that do not make sense.

    a. clap
    b. wash
    c. smell
    d. raise

Step 4: Choose the best answer.

    a. clap
    b. wash
    c. smell
    d. raise

> Check to see if the word you wrote in Step 1 is similar to the answer you circled here. They are probably very much alike!

Exercise 2

Step 1: Think about what the word means *before* you look at the answer choices.

The race car driver drove safely so that he would not <u>collide</u> with another car.

    I think <u>collide</u> means _____.

Step 2: Try each answer choice in the sentence.

The race car driver drove safely so that he would not <u>collide</u> with another car.

    a. race
    b. drift
    c. crash
    d. turn

> Don't choose your answer yet — go through all the steps!

Which of the following sentences make sense?
  1. The race car driver drove safely so that he would not <u>race</u> with another car.
     ○ yes   ○ no

  2. The race car driver drove safely so that he would not <u>drift</u> with another car.
     ○ yes   ○ no

  3. The race car driver drove safely so that he would not <u>crash</u> with another car.
     ○ yes   ○ no

  4. The race car driver drove safely so that he would not <u>turn</u> with another car.
     ○ yes   ○ no

Step 3: Cross out answer choices that do not make sense.

    a. race
    b. drift
    c. crash
    d. turn

Step 4: Choose the best answer.

  a. race
  b. drift
  c. crash
  d. turn

> Check to see if the word you wrote in Step 1 is similar to the answer you circled here. They are probably very much alike!

Exercise 3

Step 1: Think about what the word means *before* you look at the answer choices.

The doctor helped a lot of people and won a <u>monumental</u> award for her work.

  I think <u>monumental</u> means _____.

Step 2: Try each answer choice in the sentence.

The doctor helped a lot of people and won a <u>monumental</u> award for her work.
  a. great
  b. funny
  c. beautiful
  d. sick

Which of the following sentences make sense?
  1. The doctor helped a lot of people and won a <u>great</u> award for her work.
     ○ yes   ○ no

  2. The doctor helped a lot of people and won a <u>funny</u> award for her work.
     ○ yes   ○ no

  3. The doctor helped a lot of people and won a <u>beautiful</u> award for her work.
     ○ yes   ○ no

  4. The doctor helped a lot of people and won a <u>sick</u> award for her work.
     ○ yes   ○ no

Step 3: Cross out answer choices that do not make sense.

  a. great
  b. funny
  c. beautiful
  d. sick

Step 4: Choose the best answer.

  a. great
  b. funny
  c. beautiful
  d. sick

> Check to see if the word you wrote in Step 1 is similar to the answer you circled here. They are probably very much alike!

© 2013 The Critical Thinking Co.™ • www.CriticalThinking.com • 800-458-4849

Exercise 4 ⎯⎯⎯⎯⎯⎯⎯⎯⎯⎯⎯⎯⎯⎯⎯⎯⎯⎯⎯⎯⎯⎯⎯⎯⎯⎯⎯

Step 1: Think about what the word means *before* you look at the answer choices.

Bullies act as if they are brave, but really, they are <u>craven</u>.

I think <u>craven</u> means _____.

Clue: Bullies act one way, but feel another way.

Step 2: Try each answer choice in the sentence.

Bullies act as if they are brave, but really, they are <u>craven</u>.
- a. frightened
- b. happy
- c. hot
- d. silly

Which of the following sentences make sense?
1. Bullies act as if they are brave, but really, they are <u>frightened</u>.
   - ○ yes   ○ no

2. Bullies act as if they are brave, but really, they are <u>happy</u>.
   - ○ yes   ○ no

3. Bullies act as if they are brave, but really, they are <u>hot</u>.
   - ○ yes   ○ no

4. Bullies act as if they are brave, but really, they are <u>silly</u>.
   - ○ yes   ○ no

Step 3: Cross out answer choices that do not make sense.

- a. frightened
- b. happy
- c. hot
- d. silly

Step 4: Choose the best answer.

- a. frightened
- b. happy
- c. hot
- d. silly

Check to see if the word you wrote in Step 1 is similar to the answer you circled here. They are probably very much alike!

You probably feel confident about your answers because you thought carefully about each step. Even so, you can check your answers in the Answer Key on page 213.

Here are some more exercises where you will figure out what words mean. This time, there will only be <u>reminders</u> of the steps that you have already learned.

What is the definition of the underlined word in each sentence?

5. Poison dart frogs look like harmless little frogs, but they are <u>baneful</u> if other animals try to eat them.

I think <u>baneful</u> means _____.
   a. ugly
   b. cold
   c. poisonous
   d. green

Step 1: Write what the word means *before* you look at the answer choices.
Step 2: Think about how each answer choice would fit in the sentence.
Step 3: Cross out answer choices that do not make sense.
Step 4: Choose the best answer.

6. With some apples, flour, and sugar, the chef <u>rendered</u> a tasty dessert.

I think <u>rendered</u> means _____.
   a. made
   b. found
   c. bought
   d. washed

Step 1: Write what the word means *before* you look at the answer choices.
Step 2: Think about how each answer choice would fit in the sentence.
Step 3: Cross out answer choices that do not make sense.
Step 4: Choose the best answer.

7. Carlos is a <u>conscientious</u> student because he always finishes his homework.

I think <u>conscientious</u> means _____.
   a. young
   b. old
   c. talkative
   d. responsible

Step 1: Write what the word means *before* you look at the answer choices.
Step 2: Think about how each answer choice would fit in the sentence.
Step 3: Cross out answer choices that do not make sense.
Step 4: Choose the best answer.

© 2013 The Critical Thinking Co.™ • www.CriticalThinking.com • 800-458-4849

Up until now, you have been *writing* what you think the word means before you look at the answer choices. Now, that will change. You will *think* about what the word means, but you will <u>not</u> write it. When you take a test, you do not need to write as much as you do here in practice. Now that you've practiced *writing* what you think the word means, you will be much better at *thinking* about what the word means before you look at the answer choices. This kind of thinking will help you when you take a test.

What is the definition of the underlined word in each sentence?

8. The parents <u>constructed</u> a playground for the children in the neighborhood.
    a. looked at
    b. smiled at
    c. built
    d. played in

Step 1: Think about what the word means *before* you look at the answer choices.
Step 2: Think about how each answer choice would fit in the sentence.
Step 3: Cross out answer choices that do not make sense.
Step 4: Choose the best answer.

9. The baseball team was tired but <u>exuberant</u> after winning the championship game.
    a. very dirty
    b. very happy
    c. very sad
    d. very tired

Step 1: Think about what the word means *before* you look at the answer choices.
Step 2: Think about how each answer choice would fit in the sentence.
Step 3: Cross out answer choices that do not make sense.
Step 4: Choose the best answer.

10. Jack used to <u>dread</u> swimming. However, now he enjoys it because he has learned how to swim.
    a. fear
    b. practice
    c. enjoy
    d. love

Step 1: Think about what the word means *before* you look at the answer choices.
Step 2: Think about how each answer choice would fit in the sentence.
Step 3: Cross out answer choices that do not make sense.
Step 4: Choose the best answer.

What is the definition of the underlined word in each sentence? Remember to use the steps that you have learned as you figure out what each word means.

11. The book club will <u>convene</u> every Friday morning to talk about the book.
    a. read
    b. gather
    c. laugh
    d. enjoy

12. Farm animals are best suited to life in <u>rural</u> areas, but when the sheep were brought to a carnival in the city for the day, everyone, including the animals, seemed to enjoy themselves.
    a. fun
    b. noisy
    c. city
    d. country

13. Ms. Bedelia was so <u>hasty</u> when she left her house this morning that she showed up to work with two different shoes on her feet.
    a. hurried
    b. funny
    c. slow
    d. interested

© 2013 The Critical Thinking Co.™ • www.CriticalThinking.com • 800-458-4849

Sometimes on a test, you will see a blank space instead of a word. You will use the same steps to figure out which word belongs in the empty space.

Choose the word that completes each sentence.

14. In the fall, the leaves on the tree in front of the school change to a _____ color.
   a. green
   b. golden
   c. blue
   d. smart

Step 1: Think about what word belongs in the blank *before* you look at the answer choices.
Step 2: Think about how each answer choice would fit in the sentence.
Step 3: Cross out answer choices that do not make sense.
Step 4: Choose the best answer.

15. If you want to see monkeys, elephants, and other animals, then you should visit the _____.
   a. country
   b. zoo
   c. mountains
   d. pet store

Step 1: Think about what word belongs in the blank *before* you look at the answer choices.
Step 2: Think about how each answer choice would fit in the sentence.
Step 3: Cross out answer choices that do not make sense.
Step 4: Choose the best answer.

16. The circus acrobat _____ very high and then landed on top of his partner's shoulders.
   a. smiled
   b. leaped
   c. shouted
   d. waved

Step 1: Think about what word belongs in the blank *before* you look at the answer choices.
Step 2: Think about how each answer choice would fit in the sentence.
Step 3: Cross out answer choices that do not make sense.
Step 4: Choose the best answer.

17. I was so hungry that even the broccoli looked _____, and I usually don't like broccoli.
   a. delicious
   b. healthy
   c. green
   d. terrible

Step 1: Think about what word belongs in the blank *before* you look at the answer choices.
Step 2: Think about how each answer choice would fit in the sentence.
Step 3: Cross out answer choices that do not make sense.
Step 4: Choose the best answer.

Now try it without any reminders.

Choose the word that completes each sentence.

18. The mess was so _____ that Kenya thought she would
    never be able to clean it up.
    a. sad
    b. enormous
    c. fun
    d. easy

19. A backpack holds a lot of things and must be made from
    _____ material.
    a. cloth
    b. colorful
    c. easy
    d. strong

Congratulations! You have learned how to do your best when you answer questions about your vocabulary. Check your answers in the Answer Key on page 213.

If you would like to practice with more difficult questions, you can go on to the Advanced Guided Practice. However, if you would like to stop here, that is fine.

© 2013 The Critical Thinking Co.™ • www.CriticalThinking.com • 800-458-4849

Advanced Guided Practice

Use the steps to define the underlined vocabulary word in each sentence.

Step 1: Think about what the word means *before* you look at the answer choices.
Step 2: Try each answer choice in the sentence.
Step 3: Cross out answer choices that do not make sense.
Step 4: Choose the best answer.

20. Raj was so <u>engrossed</u> watching the baseball game that he forgot he had homework.
    a. rushed
    b. playful
    c. neglectful
    d. interested

21. I saw the gold dome on top of the state capitol building <u>glint</u> in the bright sunshine.
    a. heat up
    b. melt
    c. flash
    d. dance

22. Even though the <u>antique</u> piano had not been played in a century, it sounded great after it was restored.
    a. out of tune
    b. broken
    c. valuable
    d. very old

23. The climber was so <u>dogged</u> in his effort to reach the top of the mountain that he continued to climb even through a blizzard.
    a. accompanied by dogs
    b. upset
    c. determined
    d. athletic

24. Tyler's grandma _____ dessert until he finished eating his entire dinner.
    a. withheld
    b. repelled
    c. discontinued
    d. presented

Advanced Guided Practice (continued)

25. If you want to go to a place where you can see many different types of fish, seals, sharks, and other sea creatures, then you should visit the _____.
    a. ocean
    b. pet store
    c. zoo
    d. aquarium

26. The flood was a _____, forcing people to leave their homes.
    a. disaster
    b. problem
    c. hurricane
    d. tornado

© 2013 The Critical Thinking Co.™ • www.CriticalThinking.com • 800-458-4849

II. Understand the Main Idea

Everything you read has a main idea.

The main idea is the *meaning* of what you read.

On a test, if you are asked, "What was the paragraph mostly about?" you are being asked about the paragraph's main idea.

Main ideas are explained by *details*. Details are NOT the main idea, but they tell you more about the main idea.

> Do you think that you have to understand every detail of what you read a on a test? Well, you do not! All you have to understand is the main idea. You should not worry if you do not understand every detail about what you read! The exercises below will help you understand more about main ideas.

A. See the Main Idea in Pictures

These exercises will show you that you can find a main idea when you look at a **group** of pictures. They will also show you that you don't have to worry if you don't understand every detail and fact about what is in the pictures. You may not know exactly what all the pictures are, but you will still be able to find the main idea.

Exercise 1

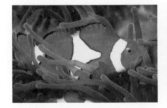

Think about how you would describe the group of pictures seen above to a friend. If you had to tell your friend the <u>main idea</u> that describes all the pictures, what would it be?

Write the main idea: _____

- If you tell one of your friends about the group of pictures seen above, you probably would NOT say, "I saw a fish, two dolphins, a shark, and a spiny lobster." Those are all details.

- You also probably don't know the exact name for each of those details. For example, you don't need to know that the creature in the last picture is called a "spiny lobster" in order to understand the main idea.

- The main idea is that the pictures show "ocean life," or "creatures that swim." Any answer that describes animals and plants that live in the ocean is correct. As long as you described the meaning of the **group** of pictures, you have stated the main idea.

© 2013 The Critical Thinking Co.™ • www.CriticalThinking.com • 800-458-4849

Write the main idea for each group of pictures.

Exercise 2

Write the main idea: _____

Exercise 3

Do you know what this is? You don't have to know! You can understand the main idea without knowing what this is. (It is called a "kiwi fruit.")

Write the main idea: _____

Exercise 4

Write the main idea: _____

          © 2013 The Critical Thinking Co.™ • www.CriticalThinking.com • 800-458-4849

B. Understand the Main Idea in a Paragraph

Just as a group of pictures can have a main idea, a paragraph is a group of sentences with a main idea. Every paragraph has a main idea. Most paragraphs also have details that support the main idea.

The next exercises will show you how to write a paragraph with a main idea and details that support the main idea.

Exercise 5

Below is a paragraph that a student (Ashley) wrote to describes the group of pictures above.

There are many types of ocean life. When most people think about ocean life, they usually think about fish. Mammals, such as dolphins, also call the ocean home. Plants, sharks, and lobsters also are part of the diverse group of living things in the ocean.

Ashley starts with a sentence that states the main idea.

There are many types of ocean life.

Then she goes on to describe details that support the main idea.

When most people think about ocean life, they usually think about fish. Mammals, such as dolphins, also call the ocean home. Plants, sharks, and lobsters also are part of the diverse group of living things in the ocean.

Exercise 6

Below is a paragraph that Ashley wrote to describe the group of pictures above.

Most people write by using a notebook with a pencil or pen.
However, there are many ways to write. More and more often,
people are writing on computers.

This time, Ashley's **second** sentence states the main idea. The main idea is that there are many ways to write. Her other sentences have details that help support the main idea.

Most people write by using a notebook with a pencil or pen.
However, there are many ways to write. More and more often,
people are writing on computers.

Exercise 7

When you were asked to write the main idea about the group of pictures seen above, you probably wrote "fruits" or "things to eat" as the main idea. Whichever you chose as the main idea is fine.

© 2013 The Critical Thinking Co.™ • www.CriticalThinking.com • 800-458-4849

Now, write a paragraph that describes the pictures.
   a. Start with a sentence that states the main idea. Some examples of a sentence stating the
        main idea are:

        • Fruits taste good.

        • There are many different types of fruits.

        • I like eating fruits.

_____

   b. Then write two or three additional sentences about the fruits. These sentences will be
        details that support the main idea.

_____

_____

_____

Exercise 8

When you were asked to write the main idea about the group of pictures above, you probably
wrote "animals" or "pets" as the main idea.   Whichever you chose as the main idea is fine.

Now, you are going to write a paragraph that describes the pictures.

Start with a sentence that states the main idea. Then write two or three additional sentences
with details about the pictures.

_____

_____

_____

_____

C. Find the Topic Sentence

In the last exercise, you wrote a paragraph. Your paragraph had a sentence that stated the main idea. A sentence that states the main idea is called a **topic sentence**. All the other sentences in your paragraph described details.

Whenever you read a paragraph on a test, if you find a topic sentence, you should underline it. You should also underline other important words and phrases (details) that will help you to understand the main idea.

Most paragraphs have a topic sentence. But sometimes the main idea is complicated, and there are many sentences that state the topic. Some paragraphs do not have a topic sentence. Even though some paragraphs do not have a topic sentence, all paragraphs have a main idea.

In the next exercises, you will read each paragraph to practice finding the topic sentence.

Exercise 9

Some people think that butterflies and moths are the same kind of insect, but they are really two different types of insects. Butterflies fly during the daytime, but moths fly at night. Butterflies have little knobs on the ends of their antennae, but moths' antennae look like feathers. Additionally, butterflies are usually more colorful than moths.

Which topic sentence states the main idea of the paragraph?
  a. Some people think that butterflies and moths are the same kind of insect, but they are really two different types of insects.
  b. Butterflies fly during the daytime, but moths fly at night.
  c. Butterflies have little knobs on the ends of their antennae, but moths' antennae look like feathers.
  d. Additionally, butterflies are usually more colorful than moths.

Remember to cross out wrong answers and then choose the best answer.

Exercise 10

I went to the water park yesterday, and I could not believe how much it had changed since last summer! A new slide was built, and it's much higher and longer than the old slide. My little brother thinks it's a scarier slide, but for an older kid like me, it's just more fun. Also, the water park now has a wave pool, which is something completely new.

Which topic sentence states the main idea of the paragraph?
  a. I went to the water park yesterday and I could not believe how much it had changed since last summer!
  b. A new slide was built, and it's much higher and longer than the old slide.
  c. My little brother thinks it's a scarier slide, but for an older kid like me, it's just more fun.
  d. Also, the water park now has a wave pool, which is something completely new.

© 2013 The Critical Thinking Co.™ • www.CriticalThinking.com • 800-458-4849

Remember that some paragraphs <u>do not</u> have a topic sentence, but they all have a main idea.

Read the paragraphs below to practice finding the main idea.

Exercise 11

A lot of kids carry everything they need for the school day in their backpacks. They carry books, notebooks, pencils, and folders. Some kids carry their lunch or at least a snack. Some kids carry a change of clothes or sneakers for sports and other activities that they do after school. With all the things that kids carry in their backpacks, it's no wonder that some kids have sore backs at the end of the day.

What is the main idea of the paragraph?
   a. Kids carry books, notebooks, pencils, and folders in their backpacks.
   b. Kids carry things in their backpacks that they will use in school.
   c. Kids carry so many things in their backpacks that it's no wonder some kids have sore backs at the end of the day.
   d. Kids like backpacks because they are colorful, fun, and sometimes have characters on them from movies and TV shows.

Exercise 12

Spiders are careful about where they spin their webs.   They seem to prefer corners. It doesn't matter if it's a corner in a fence outside or a corner inside a house. They choose corners because corners are not in the way of people or animals that might walk by and ruin the result of all their hard work. Luckily for spiders, bugs can still fly into corners and become caught in their webs.

What is the main idea of the paragraph?
   a. Spiders eat bugs that become caught in their webs.
   b. Spiders spin webs in corners because, even though bugs fly into corners, corners are not in the way of people or animals.
   c. Spiders work very hard to spin webs, but then people and animals walk by and ruin their webs.
   d. Spiders are careful and intelligent creatures.

© 2013 The Critical Thinking Co.™ • www.CriticalThinking.com • 800-458-4849

D. Think of a Good Title

Some paragraphs have **titles** above them. A good title can give you a clue about the main idea.

Let's pretend that you see a paragraph with the title **Things That Are Orange**. Even without reading the paragraph, you can guess its main idea has something to do with things that are orange.

If you read a paragraph, and you're not sure about the main idea, you can think, "What would be a good title for this paragraph?"

To choose a good title, try to find the topic sentence. If you find a topic sentence, you should use part of the topic sentence in your title.

In these next exercises, you will practice finding a good title for each paragraph.

When you read each paragraph, underline the topic sentence and other important words and phrases to help you find a good title.

Exercise 13

We have gym class every Wednesday. We learn about different sports, like basketball and volleyball. Our gym teacher, Ms. Kramer, says that gym class is not only about sports but also about any activity that keeps our bodies moving. That's why we learned about hip hop dance last week and will be jumping rope next week.

Which is the best title for the paragraph?
  a. Gym Class Is Not Only About Sports
  b. Learning About Sports in Gym Class
  c. Wednesday Gym Class
  d. Basketball in Gym Class

Exercise 14

One day in October I went to a farm that grew pumpkins. Before I arrived there, I expected to see a bunch of pumpkins sitting in rows, ready to be picked. However, when I arrived there, all I saw were a lot of very tall corn plants. I thought this was weird, because it was supposed to be a pumpkin farm. But what I learned was that the pumpkins were there, but they were hidden among the corn plants. I had to go into the field of corn plants to find the hidden pumpkins. It was more fun to find hidden pumpkins than it would have been to pick pumpkins sitting in rows out in the open.

Which is the best title for the paragraph?
  a. How to Make Pumpkin Pie
  b. All About Pumpkins
  c. Tall Corn Plants
  d. Finding Pumpkins Among Corn Plants

© 2013 The Critical Thinking Co.™ • www.CriticalThinking.com • 800-458-4849

Exercise 15

The library is supposed to be a quiet place. However, when I was there today, it was a noisy place. Kids were talking in groups, little kids were shouting, babies were crying, and parents were chatting.

Write a good title for the paragraph.

_____

Exercise 16

I want to stop taking violin lessons. I've been taking them for six months, and I really don't like learning how to play. I think that six months is enough time to figure out whether you really like something or not. I've given it a good try, and I still don't like the violin. I am willing to trade the violin for another instrument that I might like better. I have always wanted to play the guitar, and I promise to try my best if I am allowed to learn to play the guitar instead of the violin.

Write a good title for the paragraph.

_____

© 2013 The Critical Thinking Co.™ • www.CriticalThinking.com • 800-458-4849

E. Read More Than One Paragraph

So far, you have been reading just one paragraph and finding its main idea. On tests, there are times that you will have to read more than one paragraph.

Here's a secret: When you read more than one paragraph, you don't need to do anything different! You will still need to understand the main idea of each paragraph.

No matter what you read, no matter how many paragraphs it contains, <u>make sure you understand the main idea of each paragraph</u>. The better you understand the main idea of each paragraph, the better you will be able to understand the main idea from the entire passage.

What's a passage? On tests, you will read passages. A passage is a short story, a short article, or a poem. Most passages have more than one paragraph.

The passage above that you just read has three paragraphs.   1   2   3

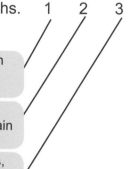

So far, you have been reading just one paragraph and finding its main idea. On tests, there are times that you will have to read more than one paragraph.

Here's a secret: When you read more than one paragraph, you don't need to do anything different! You will still need to understand the main idea from each paragraph.

No matter what you read, no matter how many paragraphs it contains, <u>make sure you understand the main idea of each paragraph</u>. The better you understand the main idea of each paragraph, the better you will be able to understand the main idea from the entire passage.

In the passages that follow, you will write the main idea of each paragraph and then choose the main idea of the whole passage.

- You will read each passage, and if you find a topic sentence, underline it as well as important words and phrases.
- Then you will write the main idea for each paragraph in the space provided.
- Finally, you will circle the letter beside the answer that best describes the main idea of the whole passage.

Some of these passages are difficult and may have words you've never heard before. Just remember, you do not need to understand every detail in the passages. You only need to understand the main idea.

© 2013 The Critical Thinking Co.™ • www.CriticalThinking.com • 800-458-4849

As you read each passage:
- Underline the topic sentence and details.
- Then write the main idea for each paragraph.
- Finally, choose which statement best describes the main idea of the passage.

Exercise 17

Along with the presidents of the United States, a lot of pets have lived at the White House. Early in White House history, most pets were farm animals. George Washington had many horses and cattle. Abraham Lincoln had ponies, rabbits, goats, and a turkey named Jip. Andrew Johnson didn't have a pet, but he left food out at night for a family of mice that lived in the White House.

This paragraph's main idea:

_____

_____

_____

In more recent years, White House pets have not been farm animals. All the recent white house pets have been cats and dogs. Bill Clinton had a cat named Socks and a dog named Buddy, who did not seem to like each other at all. George W. Bush had two mischievous Scottish terrier dogs. Barack Obama's dog, Bo, was given to him as a gift from a senator. All these White House pets have captured the imagination of American children.

This paragraph's main idea:

_____

_____

_____

What is the main idea of the **whole passage**?
- a. In the early years, most White House pets were farm animals. In recent years, they have been cats and dogs.
- b. George Washington had many horses and cattle, but Barack Obama has only one dog.
- c. Andrew Johnson didn't have a pet. However, he left food out at night for a family of mice that lived in the White House.
- d. Some of the early presidents were George Washington, Abraham Lincoln, and Andrew Johnson. Some of the more recent presidents are Bill Clinton, George W. Bush, and Barack Obama.

© 2013 The Critical Thinking Co.™ • www.CriticalThinking.com • 800-458-4849

Exercise 18

Telescopes are used by scientists to help them see things that are far away. Some of the most powerful telescopes show scientists things that are so far away that they are in other galaxies in outer space. Scientists use these powerful telescopes to study the far reaches of outer space.

This paragraph's main idea:

_____

_____

_____

Most telescopes are not as powerful as the ones that are used by scientists. Most telescopes are used by people who are not scientists, but are just curious about outer space. These telescopes can show people objects that are closer to Earth, such as the moon.

This paragraph's main idea:

_____

_____

_____

What is the main idea of the **whole passage**?
   a. Most people who use telescopes are scientists.
   b. Telescopes used by scientists are very powerful and can see far into space. Most telescopes used by people who are not scientists are not as powerful and cannot see as far.
   c. Telescopes were first used hundreds of years ago. Now, scientists do not use telescopes very often. Instead, most scientists get information about outer space from satellites.
   d. Scientists use telescopes to study the far reaches of outer space.

Congratulations! You have learned how to read a passage in a way that will help you do your best on tests. Check your answers in the Answer Key on page 213.

If you would like to practice with more difficult questions, you can go on to the Advanced Guided Practice. However, if you would like to stop here, that is fine.

© 2013 The Critical Thinking Co.™ • www.CriticalThinking.com • 800-458-4849

Advanced Guided Practice

Read each of the passages and answer the questions.

Exercise 19

One of the best things about drawing and coloring is choosing the colors that you will use. Drawing and coloring with a small box of crayons is okay, but using a really big box of crayons is much more fun. A small box of crayons usually has one red crayon, but a big box of crayons not only has one red crayon, but also has other types of red crayons like "brick red," "strawberry red," and "red violet." Having a bunch of different reds to choose from is a whole lot more fun than having just one. Also, the crayons in a small box wear out quickly, but the crayons in a big box seem to last longer. It's more fun when crayons last a long time.

What is the topic sentence?
a. One of the best things about drawing and coloring is choosing the colors that you will use.
b. Drawing and coloring with a small box of crayons is okay, but using a really big box of crayons is much more fun.
c. A small box of crayons usually has one red crayon, but a big box of crayons not only has one red crayon, but also has other types of red crayons like "brick red," "strawberry red," and "red violet."
d. Also, the crayons in a small box wear out quickly, but the crayons in a big box seem to last longer.

Exercise 20

Wild horses are usually smaller than domestic horses. The food they eat in the wild isn't as nutritious as the food that domestic horses eat on farms. This makes wild horses grow less tall than domestic horses. Oddly, for wild horses, this shorter stature is a good thing. Their legs are shorter than those of domestic horses, but they are sturdier and stronger than those of domestic horses. This helps wild horses live in rough, wild terrain without hurting their legs. Many domestic horses, with their longer, less sturdy legs, would not be able to climb mountain passes or cross over unstable ground without breaking a leg if they were to slip.

Which is the best title for the paragraph?
a. For Wild Horses, Short Legs Are a Good Thing
b. For Domestic Horses, Long Legs Are a Good Thing
c. Why Wild Horses Are Smaller Than Domestic Horses
d. Climbing Mountain Passes Is Easy for Wild Horses

Advanced Guided Practice (continued)

Exercise 21

Your eyes are delicate. For this reason, your eyes must be protected. Your eyelids offer great protection for your eyes. Whenever a piece of dust flies in your eye, you blink your eyelids in order to get it out. You also blink in order to keep your eyes moist. Eyelids help moisten your eyes with a small amount of tears every time you blink. Whenever you go out in the bright sun, your eyelids can protect your eyes from the brightness and the strong rays. For more protection, you can always help your eyelids by wearing sunglasses and a hat when you go outside.

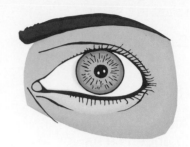

Write a good title for the paragraph.

_____

Exercise 22

Saturday morning had come, and Becky felt cheerful. The fall was bright and fresh. Leaves covered the yard and looked like a beautiful carpet of fall colors.

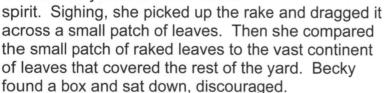

This paragraph's main idea:

_____

_____

Then Becky saw the rake. Her little brother had carried it from the garage and placed it down before her. Becky surveyed the carpet of leaves and all gladness left her, as a melancholy settled down on her spirit. Sighing, she picked up the rake and dragged it across a small patch of leaves. Then she compared the small patch of raked leaves to the vast continent of leaves that covered the rest of the yard. Becky found a box and sat down, discouraged.

This paragraph's main idea:

_____

_____

_____

The second paragraph has a lot of words in it that you may not have heard before, like "surveyed," "melancholy," and "vast continent."

Even if you don't understand the meaning of every word, you can still understand the main idea.

What is the main idea of the **whole passage**?
  a. Becky felt cheerful that it was a nice fall day, but then felt discouraged about all the leaves she had to rake.
  b. Fall leaves can look beautiful, but they are no fun to rake.
  c. Becky was having a great morning until her little brother started to bother her.
  d. Becky felt cheerful, but later felt discouraged.

© 2013 The Critical Thinking Co.™ • www.CriticalThinking.com • 800-458-4849

III. Answer Multiple Choice Questions

You have learned how to read a passage and understand the main idea. Now, you will practice reading passages and answering multiple choice questions about what you have read using the following steps.

Step 1: Look at the questions before you read the passage. Read only the questions, not the answer choices.

Read the questions, NOT the answer choices.

After you quickly read the questions, you will know what words and phrases (details) are important to underline as you read the passage.

Step 2: Read the passage ONCE to understand the main idea. Underline important details.

You have learned that you don't need to know the meaning of every detail.

When you take a test, you probably will not understand every word in a passage, and you may not understand the meaning of every detail. This is normal. You don't have to understand every part of what you read.

The only thing you must understand is the main idea. The best practice for understanding the main idea is to read the passage only ONCE. You should underline any details about the main idea and anything that you remember from having read the questions.

You can always reread the passage later, as you answer the questions.

"After I look at the questions, I'll read the passage ONCE to understand the main idea. I won't worry if I don't understand all the details. I can always read the passage again when I answer the questions."

Step 3: Reread the underlined details if you need help to answer the questions.

When you go back to reread a passage, the parts that you underlined will help you to focus your reading. You do not need to read the whole passage again! You should only read the underlined words of the passage that will help you answer the questions.

Step 4: Cross out the wrong answers, and then choose the best answer.

Remember when you did this in the Vocabulary section? For every multiple choice question, you can cross out wrong answers, and then choose the best answer.

Even though you've read about the steps, you will understand how to use them only after you practice a few times. In the Guided Practice, you'll read passages and answer multiple choice questions step by step.

© 2013 The Critical Thinking Co.™ • www.CriticalThinking.com • 800-458-4849

Guided Practice

You just learned these four steps that will help you answer multiple choice questions:

Step 1: Look at the questions before you read the passage. Read only the question, not the answer choices.

Step 2: Read the passage once to understand the main idea. Underline important details.

Step 3: Reread the underlined details if you need help to answer the questions.

Step 4: Cross out the wrong answers, and then choose the best answer.

Now you will practice each of the steps in the next exercises. These exercises guide you through each step. After you practice, you will feel more confident when you answer multiple choice questions. The first exercise is partially completed for you.

Exercise 1

Step 1: Read the questions.

Read the questions, not the answer choices. (On a test, questions would follow the passage.)

1. Why is it important that polar bears have black skin?
2. About how much does an adult polar bear weigh?
3. The passage states that polar bears hunt which animals?
4. What is the main idea of the passage?

Step 2: Read the passage once to understand the main idea. Underline important details.

Underline anything that you remember from reading the questions.

Polar Bears

If you like cute baby animals, one of the very cutest is the baby polar bear, with its cuddly white fur. However, look out, that cute bear cub will grow into a ferocious adult bear who might <u>weigh about 1,000 pounds</u>. <u>Adult polar bears are hunters</u> who use their white fur to hide from their prey in the snowy Arctic. White fur helps polar bears when they <u>hunt</u> because <u>seals</u> and other animals cannot see them coming.

Something you might not know about polar bears is that even though their fur is white, the skin underneath their fur is black. <u>Black skin absorbs sunlight</u> to help the bears keep warm. It's important that polar bears are able to keep warm because they live in the coldest place on Earth.

© 2013 The Critical Thinking Co.™ • www.CriticalThinking.com • 800-458-4849

Step 3: Reread the underlined details to help you answer the questions.

Use what you have underlined to help focus your reading.

Step 4: Cross out the wrong answers, and then choose the best answer.

1. Why is it important that polar bears have black skin?
    a. ~~Because white fur looks good with black skin.~~
    (b.) Because black skin absorbs sunlight to help the bears keep warm.
    c. ~~Because black skin helps the bears hunt.~~
    d. ~~It is not important that polar bears have black skin.~~

2. About how much does an adult polar bear weigh?
    a. 200 pounds
    b. 500 pounds
    c. 1,000 pounds
    d. 2,000 pounds

3. The passage states that polar bears hunt which animal?
    a. seals
    b. fish
    c. chickens
    d. sharks

4. What is the main idea of the passage?
    a. Polar bears have fur and skin that help them survive.
    b. Polar bears are cute and cuddly.
    c. Polar bears are good hunters.
    d. Polar bears wish that they could live in a warmer place.

Exercise 2

Step 1: Read the questions (on the next page).

Read the questions, not the answer choices.

Step 2: Read the passage once to understand the main idea. Underline important details.

Underline anything that you remember from reading the questions.

Dear Principal Brady

Dear Principal Brady,

Another school in our area, the Hawthorne School, is having a field day on Friday, May 8. The students and teachers will be spending the school day outside. They will have relay races, play kickball, and sing songs they learned in music class.

I think that a field day would be a good idea for Strauss Elementary. It will give us a chance to exercise. If we sing, we can show what we learned in music class. Best of all, it will be a fun celebration for the end of the school year.

Please consider having a field day.

Sincerely,
Sean Taylor

Step 3: Reread the underlined details to help you answer the questions.

Use what you have underlined to help focus your reading.

© 2013 The Critical Thinking Co.™ • www.CriticalThinking.com • 800-458-4849

Step 4: Cross out the wrong answers, and then choose the best answer.

5. Sean Taylor, the student who wrote the letter, writes that the **best** reason to have a field day is because:
    a. it will be a fun celebration for the end of the school year.
    b. it will give students a chance to exercise.
    c. it will give students a chance to sing and show what they learned in music class.
    d. it will be a time when students and teachers can spend the school day outside.

6. What is the name of Sean's school?
    a. Hawthorne Elementary
    b. the Hawthorne School
    c. Strauss Elementary
    d. The letter does not state the name of the school.

7. Which field day activity was **not** mentioned in Sean's letter?
    a. relay races
    b. kickball
    c. singing songs
    d. eating lunch

© 2013 The Critical Thinking Co.™ • www.CriticalThinking.com • 800-458-4849

Exercise 3

Step 1: Read the questions (on the next page).

Read the questions, not the answer choices.

Step 2: Read the passage once to understand the main idea. Underline important details.

Underline anything that you remember from having read the questions.

How to Make French Toast

French toast is not just for people who live in France! It's popular all around the world because it is delicious and doesn't take much time to make. Here's how to make French toast.

<u>What You Will Need</u>
    a medium-sized bowl
    2 eggs
    ¼ cup of milk
    a dash of cinnamon
    4 slices of bread or 2 slices of Texas toast bread
    a frying pan
    a tablespoon of butter
    Note: Texas toast bread is exactly the same as other bread, except the loaves
            are bigger, and the slices are thicker.

<u>What to Do</u>
Crack the eggs into the medium-sized bowl. Add the milk and cinnamon. Stir with a fork or a wire whisk.

Soak the slices of bread in the mixture in the bowl. Four slices of bread will soak up all the eggs, milk, and cinnamon. If you use Texas toast bread, only 2 slices will soak up the ingredients.

Place the pan on a stove and heat to medium-high. You will need help from an adult as you work over a hot stove. Place the butter in the pan, and when it is melted, put the soaked bread slices in the pan. Cook for about two minutes, then flip the bread over with a spatula. After another two minutes, remove the toast from the pan. Your French toast is done!

Put your French toast on a plate, and serve it with your choice of toppings. Some delicious topping choices are maple syrup, whipped cream, and blueberries.

© 2013 The Critical Thinking Co.™ • www.CriticalThinking.com • 800-458-4849

Step 3: Reread the underlined details to help you answer the questions.

Use what you have underlined to help focus your reading.

Step 4: Cross out the wrong answers, and then choose the best answer.

8. According to this recipe, French toast is popular all around the world because:
    a. it can be served with your choice of toppings.
    b. it is delicious and doesn't take much time to make.
    c. it comes from France.
    d. it comes from Texas.

9. When you follow the directions, what do you do <u>right after</u> you crack the eggs into the medium-sized bowl?
    a. Add the milk and cinnamon.
    b. Stir vigorously with a fork or a wire whisk.
    c. Soak the slices of bread in the mixture in the bowl.
    d. Place the pan on a stove and heat to medium-high.

10. How is Texas toast bread different from other types of bread?
    a. Texas toast bread should never be used for making French toast.
    b. Texas toast bread is exactly the same as any other type of bread.
    c. Texas toast bread is exactly the same as any other type of bread, except the loaves are bigger, and the slices are thicker.
    d. Texas toast bread tastes better than any other type of bread.

11. The most important reason why you may need help from an adult when you make French toast is because:
    a. stirring the ingredients is very messy.
    b. kids aren't able to crack eggs very well.
    c. you will need help to reach all the ingredients in the cabinets.
    d. you will need help as you work over a hot stove.

Congratulations! You have learned how to read a passage in a way that will help you do your best when you answer multiple choice questions. Check your answers in the Answer Key on page 214.

If you would like to practice with more difficult questions, you can go on to the Advanced Guided Practice. However, if you would like to stop here, that is fine.

Advanced Guided Practice

Use the steps to answer the multiple choice questions.

> **Step 1**: Read the questions.
> **Step 2**: Read the passage once to understand the main idea. Underline important details.
> **Step 3**: Reread the underlined details to help you answer the questions.
> **Step 4**: Cross out the wrong answers, and then choose the best answer.

Exercise 4

The Olympic Flame

What Is the Olympic Flame?

At the Olympic Games, athletes from all over the world come together to compete in sports like basketball, volleyball, figure skating, swimming, and many, many others. The Olympic Games offer great sporting events, but the Olympics offer more than just sports. The Olympic Games offer a chance to be inspired by athletes from many different countries who come together to compete and show respect for one another. The spirit of fair competition and respect is symbolized at the Olympic Games by the Olympic flame.

During the weeks that the Olympic Games are held, the Olympic flame burns in a big bowl, called a cauldron. Back in ancient times, the Olympics were held in Greece, and a flame burned in a cauldron during the weeks that the Olympics were being held. Even back then, the flame celebrated the Olympic spirit of fair competition and respect among athletes.

Carrying the Olympic Flame From Greece

The Olympic Games are no longer held only in Greece, as had been done in ancient times, but are now held in different cities all over the world. At every Olympics, a cauldron burns with the Olympic flame. It would make sense to light the Olympic flame in the cauldron with a match, just like someone might light a big candle. However, it is not done this way. It is done in a way that is more complicated but also more fun and more meaningful. The Olympic flame is ignited, or started, in Greece, where the games were first held. Then that flame is carried all the way from Greece to wherever the Olympic Games are being held. For example, when the Olympic Games were held in Beijing, China, the flame was ignited in Greece and was carried all the way from Greece to China.

Carrying the Olympic flame takes a few weeks, or a few months, depending on how far it has to travel. Usually, a runner carries the flame with a torch. The flaming torch is passed from one runner to another runner, and then again and again through a succession of runners, until it reaches the final destination, which is the place where the Olympics are held.

Although the torch is usually carried by runners, it has also been carried in many other ways. The torch has been carried across oceans in boats and has flown in airplanes. It also has been carried by canoe, by someone riding on a camel, and even by divers under the ocean water! When the flame was taken under water, it had to be kept inside a special box so that it would not be put out by the water.

© 2013 The Critical Thinking Co.™ • www.CriticalThinking.com • 800-458-4849

Lighting the Cauldron With the Olympic Flame

After the torch has made its long journey from Greece, it finally arrives in the city where the Olympics are to be held. At the start of the Olympics, there is a great ceremony, where thousands of the world's best athletes march into a big stadium. After the athletes have arrived in the stadium, the Olympic cauldron is finally lit by the torch. The person who is the last to run with the torch has the honor of lighting the cauldron with the Olympic flame. Usually that person is a famous athlete from the country where the Olympics are being held. Sometimes, that person is not famous at all, but rather, a person who represents the spirit of the Olympics. For example, in 1988, a 12-year-old figure skater lit the Olympic cauldron because she symbolized the future of the Olympic spirit. No matter who lights the Olympic flame, it is always done to celebrate not only the sports, but also to celebrate fair competition and respect that is the spirit of the Olympic Games.

12. The Olympic flame:
    a. is the same thing as the Olympic torch.
    b. is the same thing as the Olympic cauldron.
    c. can burn in a torch or in a cauldron.
    d. always burns in a cauldron.

13. The chart below shows main ideas from the passage. Which sentence belongs in the third box?

The Olympic flame is a symbol of the Olympic spirit of competition and respect.	The Olympic flame is carried from Greece to wherever the Olympic Games are held.	?

    a. The Olympic flame has been carried in many interesting ways.
    b. Carrying the Olympic flame takes a few weeks, or a few months, depending on how far it has to travel.
    c. At the start of the Olympics, there is a great ceremony, where thousands of athletes from all over the world march in to a big stadium.
    d. The Olympic flame is used to light a cauldron at the ceremony that starts the Olympic Games.

© 2013 The Critical Thinking Co.™ • www.CriticalThinking.com • 800-458-4849

14. The most common way that the Olympic flame is carried is by:
   a. a runner.
   b. someone riding a camel.
   c. someone on a boat.
   d. an ocean diver.

15. According to the passage, the Olympic flame burns while the Olympics are being held because the flame:
   a. reminds people of ancient Greece.
   b. is a symbol of the Olympic spirit.
   c. tells people that the Olympics are being held.
   d. tells people where they can see the Olympics.

16. According to the passage, the Olympic spirit is the spirit of:
   a. the Olympic flame.
   b. the Olympic cauldron.
   c. fair competition and respect for others.
   d. famous athletes playing sports.

17. Read this sentence from the passage:
   The flaming torch is passed from one runner to another runner, and then again and again through a <u>succession</u> of runners, until it reaches the final destination, which is the place where the Olympics are held.

   The word <u>succession</u> probably means:
   a. line.
   b. torch.
   c. crowd.
   d. success.

> On a test you will often be asked about the meaning of words. Use the steps that you have learned in the Vocabulary section in order to figure out what the vocabulary word <u>succession</u> means.
> **Step 1:** Think about what the word means *before* you look at the answer choices.
> **Step 2:** Try each answer choice in the sentence.
> **Step 3:** Cross out answer choices that do not make sense.
> **Step 4:** Choose the best answer.

© 2013 The Critical Thinking Co.™ • www.CriticalThinking.com • 800-458-4849

Exercise 5 ———————————————————————————————

The Science of Being Ticklish

When someone tickles you, the nerve endings under your skin feel the light movement, and it feels funny. Some parts of your body have more nerve endings than others. For example, the soles of your feet have more nerve endings than your ankles, and that's why the soles of your feet are more ticklish than your ankles.

When someone tickles you, you usually feel a little uncomfortable, but the slight discomfort can make you laugh. That's what being ticklish actually is—slight discomfort.

One thing you may have noticed is that you cannot tickle yourself. Go ahead and try it. Are you laughing? You probably are not. Scientists explain that when we tickle ourselves, our brains already know what is going to happen, and so we don't laugh from the feeling of being tickled. Scientists think that if you're not surprised by the light movement, then you don't feel the slight discomfort that makes you feel tickled. So, it may be that the reason you cannot tickle yourself is because you cannot surprise yourself. Part of the slight discomfort that you feel when you are tickled comes not only from feeling the light movement, but also from being surprised by the light movement.

Scientists have found that a region of the brain called the cerebellum is what prevents us from tickling ourselves. The cerebellum can distinguish sensations that we make by our own movements, like tickling ourselves, from sensations that come from other people and things, like someone else tickling us. The cerebellum makes the brain disregard sensations that we make ourselves, while it helps us pay attention when someone or something else touches us. For example, the cerebellum helps you disregard the sensation you feel while you fold your own arms together, but pay a lot of attention if someone else touches you on the shoulder. The difference in your reactions to movements and sensations that you make yourself, and those that come from other people and things, is actually very useful. It's not important for you to react if you touch your own arm, but it is very important for you to react if someone else touches your arm, or if a bug crawls on your arm!

It's a great thing that our cerebellum allows us to disregard the sensations that come from our own movements. Imagine how annoying it would be to feel touched and tickled all day long! You can thank your cerebellum for saving you a lot of discomfort. Also, when you do have fun laughing when someone else tickles you, you can thank your cerebellum for that too.

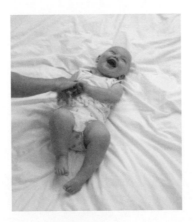

18. According to the passage, what is the best reason why the soles of your feet are more ticklish than your ankles?
    a. Feet are farther from the brain than ankles.
    b. Feet have more nerve endings than ankles.
    c. Feet are not capable of feeling slight discomfort as intensely as ankles.
    d. It is more surprising when you feel slight movement on your feet than when you feel slight movement on your ankles.

19. According to the passage, you cannot tickle yourself because:
    a. you cannot cause yourself to feel slight discomfort.
    b. you cannot feel anything if you tickle yourself.
    c. you cannot surprise yourself with your own movements.
    d. your cerebellum helps you to pay close attention to movements that are made by other people and things.

20. According to the passage, it is important that you are able to disregard the sensations that come from your own movements. If you could **not** disregard the sensations that come from your own movements, then:
    a. you would not be able to react if someone else touched your shoulder, or if a bug crawled on your arm.
    b. you would be very annoyed because you would feel touched and tickled all day long.
    c. you would not be able to laugh if someone else tickled you.
    d. you would not be surprised by any light movement.

© 2013 The Critical Thinking Co.™ • www.CriticalThinking.com • 800-458-4849

IV. Give Written Answers

Most questions on tests are multiple choice questions. However, you may be asked to write a short answer to a question.

Some kids feel nervous about writing. The teachers who will read your answers just want you to explain things to them. That's all. They are not impressed with fancy writing. They are not impressed with big words. They just want you to explain your answer clearly.

The best way to explain your answer clearly is to <u>answer the question as if you are explaining it to someone who does not understand the question or the passage at all</u>.

"Let's pretend that I don't know anything about the questions or the passage. Explain these things to me!"

Whenever you read a passage on a test, follow the steps that you learned in Section 3: Multiple Choice Questions.

Step 1: Read the questions.
Step 2: Read the passage once to understand the main idea. Underline important details.
Step 3: Reread the passage if you need help to answer the questions.

However, when you are asked to **write** an answer, Step 4 will explain how to do this.

Step 4: Write the answer in your own words.

    a. Restate the question.

> When you **restate** something, you say it again, only using different words.
> When you restate the question, you will repeat some of the words and phrases in the question. This shows that you understand the question.
>
> For example:
>   Question: What is the main idea of the passage?
>   Restated: The main idea of the passage is …

    b. Add specific information from the passage that describes the main idea.

> When you add information from the passage, you **show exactly how something from the passage answers the question**. You should **be specific.** You should use specific names of characters, places, and things that are in the passage. You should not use pronouns such as "she," " he," or "it," because it could be unclear who you are talking about.

    c. State your own thoughts if you think it will help you to explain your answer.

> **Sometimes stating your own thoughts will help you to explain your answer**. Also, if the question asks you what you think, you will need to state your own thoughts.

You will practice each of these steps and give written answers in the Guided Practice.

© 2013 The Critical Thinking Co.™ • www.CriticalThinking.com • 800-458-4849

Guided Practice

The best way to learn how to write answers is to practice.

> **Step 1:** Read the questions.
> **Step 2:** Read the passage once to understand the main idea. Underline important details.
> **Step 3:** Reread the passage if you need help to answer the questions.
> **Step 4:** Write the answer in your own words.
>   a. Restate the question.
>   b. Add specific information from the passage.
>   c. State your own thoughts if you think it will help you to explain your answers.

Here you will read passages and then write answers to questions. You should use the steps as a guide. The first exercise is partially completed for you.

Exercise 1

Step 1: Read the questions. (On a test, questions would follow the passage.)

1. What is the main idea of the passage?
2. Explain a detail from the passage that supports the main idea.

Step 2: Read the passage once to understand the main idea. Underline important details.

Underline anything that you remember from reading the questions.

An Elephant's Trunk

An <u>elephant's trunk is a nose</u> that is used for <u>more than breathing and smelling</u>. Elephants can <u>suck up water</u> with their trunks and then squirt the water in their mouths to drink or squirt the water on their backs to take a shower. You cannot do that with your own nose! Elephants can also use their trunks much like people use their hands. Elephants can pick up food with their trunks and then bring it to their mouths to eat, much like you would pick up your food with your hands and bring it to your mouth to eat. Elephants also <u>say "hello" to each other</u> by touching <u>their trunks together</u>, much like people shaking hands. Elephants are animals with remarkable noses.

Step 3: Reread the passage if you need help to answer the questions.

Use what you have underlined to help focus your reading.

© 2013 The Critical Thinking Co.™ • www.CriticalThinking.com • 800-458-4849

Step 4: Write the answers in your own words.

1. What is the main idea of the passage?

    a. Restate the question.

    The main idea of the passage is that _____

_____

_____

    b. Add specific information from the passage that describes the main idea.

_____

_____

_____

    c. State your own thoughts if you think it will help you to explain your answer.

_____

_____

_____

2. Explain a detail from the passage that supports the main idea.

    a. Restate the question.

_____

_____

_____

    b. Add specific information from the passage that describes the main idea.

_____

_____

_____

    c. State your own thoughts if you think it will help you to explain your answer.

_____

_____

_____

Now that you have answered the questions, you probably want to know how well you've done. There are many good answers to these questions.

To help you with your answers, you can see how someone else (Sophia) answered the questions.

Sophia's written answer to the first question is below.

1. What is the main idea of the passage?

     An elephant's trunk is a nose that is used for many things.

     _____

     _____

Sophia's answer is good, but it could better. Here's how she can improve her answer:

   a. Restate the question.

     The main idea of the passage is that an elephant's trunk is a nose used for

     many things.

     _____

In red you can see that Sophia restated the question. Now the reader knows that she understands the question.

   b. Add specific information from the passage that describes the main idea.

     The main idea of the passage is that an elephant's trunk is a nose used for

     ~~many things~~ more than breathing and smelling.

     _____

Sophia crossed out "many things." Instead, in red, you can see that she used **more specific** words from the passage.

Your answer does not need to be exactly like Sophia's in order to be correct. As long as you have restated the question and have used specific details in the passage that answer the question, you have written a good answer.

© 2013 The Critical Thinking Co.™ • www.CriticalThinking.com • 800-458-4849

Sophia's written answer to the second question is below.

2. Explain a detail from the passage that supports the main idea.

Elephants touch their trunks together to say "hello" to each other.

Sophia's answer is good, but it could better. Here's how she can improve her answer:

a. Restate the question.

A detail that supports the main idea is that elephants touch their trunks together to say "hello" to each other.

In red you can see that Sophia restated the question. Now the reader knows that she understands the question.

b. Add specific information from the passage that describes the main idea.

A detail that supports the main idea is that elephants touch their trunks together to say "hello" to each other.

Sophia has done well using specific information from the passage. She does not need to add any more specific information.

c. State your own thoughts if you think it will help you to explain your answer.

A detail that supports the main idea is that elephants touch their trunks together to say "hello" to each other. This detail shows that elephants use their trunks for more than just breathing and smelling.

Sophia has already used specific information from the passage. Next, in red, she states her own thoughts. She explains how the detail supports the main idea.

Now her answer is not just good, it's great!

Your answer does not need to be exactly like Sophia's in order to be correct. You may have chosen to discuss a different detail, such as elephants using their trunks to drink, take a shower, or pick up food.

Exercise 2

Step 1: Read the questions. (On a test, questions would follow the passage.)

3. What is the main idea of the passage?

4. Pretend that you are a judge of a pet costume contest. You have decided that the winner is a cute little kitten dressed as if it were a tough and powerful superhero. Explain your choice.

Step 2: Read the passage once to understand the main idea. Underline important details.

Underline anything that you remember from having read the questions.

Pet Costume Contests

A new tradition has taken hold: contests for pets in costume. No one is sure how it started, but many communities hold pet costume contests as a regular part of celebrating the fall.

No pet is excluded from this tradition. At one contest in Baltimore, Maryland, several goldfish turned out with each of their bowls decorated as different colored gumballs. They were placed in a small bookcase and were surrounded with plastic casing to make them look as if they were in a gumball machine. The originality and creativity of the "goldfish gumball machine" took first prize.

Sometimes it's not originality and creativity that takes the prize. Sometimes it's humor. There are many contests where the judges cannot resist a tough looking bulldog dressed in a dainty ballerina costume. A "bulldog ballerina" is unexpected and funny. Another classic winner is a pair of animals dressed as a bride and groom. Whether these contests celebrate creativity or just humor, pet costume contests are a welcome new tradition.

Step 3: Reread the passage if you need help to answer the questions.

Use what you have underlined to help focus your reading.

Step 4: Write the answer in your own words.

    a. Restate the question.
    b. Add specific information from the passage.
    c. State your own thoughts if you think it will help you to explain your answer.

3. What is the main idea of the passage?

    a. Restate the question.

_____

_____

_____

© 2013 The Critical Thinking Co.™ • www.CriticalThinking.com • 800-458-4849

b. Add information from the passage that describes the main idea.

_____

_____

_____

c. State your own thoughts if you think it will help you to explain your answer.

_____

_____

_____

4. Pretend that you are a judge of a pet costume contest. You have decided that the winner is a cute little kitten dressed as if it were a tough and powerful superhero. Explain your choice.

a. Restate the question.

You also may have to use some words in the sentence **before** the question:

<u>If I were a judge of a pet costume contest, I would choose a cute little kitten</u>

<u>dressed as a tough and powerful superhero because</u> _____

_____

b. As you explain your choice, be sure to use specific information from the passage.

_____

_____

_____

c. State your own thoughts if you think it will help you to explain your answer.

_____

_____

_____

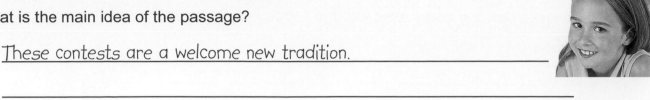

Here is Sophia's answer to the third question:

3. What is the main idea of the passage?

These contests are a welcome new tradition.

Sophia's answer is good, but it could better. Here's how she can improve her answer:

a. Restate the question.

The main idea of the passage is that these contests are a welcome new tradition.

In red you can see that Sophia restated the question.

b. Add specific information from the passage.

The main idea of the passage is that ~~these~~ pet costume contests are a welcome new tradition.

Sophia crossed out the word "these." She replaced "these" with specific words in red, which were in the passage. Now the reader knows exactly what she is talking about.

c. State your own thoughts if you think it will help you to explain your answer.

The main idea of the passage is that pet costume contests are a welcome new tradition. All kinds of pets can be dressed up and entered in contests.

Even though her answer is pretty clear, Sophia has decided to add one of her own thoughts. In red you can see that Sophia has written a little more about the main idea of the passage.

Your answer does not need to be exactly like Sophia's in order to be correct. As long as you have restated the question and have discussed specific information from the passage that answers the question, you have written a good answer.   Even though Sophia chose to state her own thoughts, you do not have to do this if you feel as though your answer is already clear.

© 2013 The Critical Thinking Co.™ • www.CriticalThinking.com • 800-458-4849

Here is Sophia's answer to the fourth question:

4. Pretend that you are a judge of a pet costume contest. You have decided that the winner is a cute little kitten dressed as if it were a tough and powerful superhero. Explain your choice.

   a. Restate the question.

   I chose the kitten dressed as if it were a tough and powerful superhero
   because it is cute and funny.

   _____

Sophia's answer is good, but it could be better. Here's how she can improve her answer:

Sophia has already restated part of the question. To be clearer, she can restate even more of the question. In red you can see that Sophia added even more words from the question.

   If I were a judge of a pet costume contest, I would choose the kitten
   dressed as if it were a tough and powerful superhero because it is cute
   and funny.

   b. Add specific information from the passage.

   c. State your own thoughts if you think it will help you to explain your answer.

   If I were a judge of a pet costume contest, I would choose the kitten
   dressed as if it were a tough and powerful superhero because it is cute
   and funny. No one expects to see a cute little kitten dressed up as if it
   were tough and powerful. This is unexpected and funny, and that is why
   it is the winner of the contest.

As she states her own thoughts, she can add even more information from the passage. In red you can see that Sophia added even more information from the passage as she stated her own thoughts.

"Sophia's answer is great because I can understand her answer even if I have not read the question or the passage."

Exercise 3

Step 1: Read the questions. (On a test, questions would follow the passage.)

5. What are the three things that you should do if your clothes catch fire?
6. Why is it a bad idea to run if your clothes catch fire?
7. Why do firefighters think that kids are great fire safety teachers?
8. According to the passage, what is a simple thing that can save many lives?

Step 2: Read the passage once to understand the main idea. Underline important details.

Underline anything that you remember from having previewed the questions.

Kids Are Great Fire Safety Teachers

Many firefighters say that kids are great fire safety teachers. Why? Firefighters teach kids about fire safety in schools and in community centers, and then, kids go home and teach their parents and the rest of their families about fire safety. So when firefighters teach kids about fire safety, they can count on those kids to go home and teach many more people about fire safety.

One thing that firefighters teach kids in fire safety programs is what to do if their clothes catch fire. If your clothes ever catch fire, it is a scary thing. What should you do? First, you should STOP. You should never run! Next, you should DROP to the floor. Finally, you should ROLL around on the floor. Rolling around on the floor puts the fire out. Fire needs oxygen from the air, but if you roll around, the fire cannot get much air, and you will put the fire out. However, if you run, then the fire will burn stronger, because running only gives the fire more oxygen to grow. So, firefighters teach kids how to STOP, DROP, and ROLL if their clothes ever catch fire. Then, of course, kids go home and teach the rest of their families how to STOP, DROP, and ROLL if they see that their clothes are on fire.

STOP, DROP, and ROLL is an important fire safety rule that kids learn from firefighters and then teach to their families. Perhaps more important is something even simpler. Fire fighters teach kids about the importance of having smoke alarms in homes and about the importance of making sure that those smoke alarms work properly. Firefighters say that many lives are saved when kids remind their parents to check the smoke alarms in their homes.

So if you think that firefighters are great fire safety teachers, you are only partially right. Kids are great fire safety teachers, too. Tell your parents to check the smoke alarms in your home today!

Step 3: Reread the passage if you need help to answer the questions.

Use what you have underlined to help focus your reading.

© 2013 The Critical Thinking Co.™ • www.CriticalThinking.com • 800-458-4849

Step 4: Write the answer in your own words.

    a. Restate the question.
    b. Add specific information from the passage.
    c. State your own thoughts if you think it will help you to explain your answer.

5. What are the three things that you should do if your clothes catch fire?

_____

_____

_____

_____

6. Why is it a bad idea to run if your clothes catch fire?

_____

_____

_____

_____

5. What are the three things that you should do if your clothes catch fire?

Below is an example of how Sophia answered the questions.
The answers that you gave will probably not be exactly like her answers, and that's okay.

The three things that you should do if your clothes catch fire are STOP,

DROP, and ROLL.

Here is another way to answer the question. You will see that this answer adds even more
specific information from the passage.

The three things that you should do if your clothes catch fire are STOP,

DROP, and ROLL. This means that you should stop what you're doing,

drop to the floor, and roll around because this will make the fire go out.

6. Why is it a bad idea to run if your clothes catch fire?

Below is an example of how Sophia answered the question.
The answer that you gave will probably not be exactly like her answer, and that's okay.

It is a bad idea to run if your clothes catch fire because if you run, the

fire will only get worse.

Here is another answer that adds even more specific information:

It is a bad idea to run if your clothes catch fire because if you run, the

fire will only get worse. Running gives the fire more oxygen and makes

the fire get worse.

© 2013 The Critical Thinking Co.™ • www.CriticalThinking.com • 800-458-4849

Here are the last two questions about fire safety. You can reread the passage before answering the questions. Remember to use step 4 below.

Step 4: Write the answer in your own words.

    a. Restate the question.
    b. Add specific information from the passage.
    c. State your own thoughts if you think it will help you to explain your answer.

7. Why do firefighters think that kids are great fire safety teachers?

_____

_____

_____

_____

8. According to the passage, what is a simple thing that can save many lives?

_____

_____

_____

_____

Below are examples of how Sophia answered the questions.
The answers that you gave will probably not be exactly like her answers, and that's okay.

7. Why do firefighters think that kids are great fire safety teachers?

Firefighters think that kids are great fire safety teachers because kids go home and tell their families everything that they learn from fire fighters in fire safety classes.

Here is another answer that adds even more specific information:

Firefighters think that kids are great fire safety teachers because kids go home and tell their families everything that they learn from fire fighters in fire safety classes. Firefighters count on kids to teach their families about fire safety.

This sentence states the student's own thoughts.

8. According to the passage, what is a simple thing that can save many lives?

According to the passage, a simple thing that can save many lives is to check the smoke alarms in your home.

Here is another answer that adds even more specific information:

According to the passage, a simple thing that can save many lives is to check the smoke alarms in your home. It is important to make sure that the smoke alarms work. If they do not work, then they cannot tell you to get out of your home if there's a fire.

Congratulations! You have learned how to write good answers to test questions.

If you would like to practice with more difficult questions, you can go on to Advanced Guided Practice. If you would like to stop here, that is fine.

© 2013 The Critical Thinking Co.™ • www.CriticalThinking.com • 800-458-4849

Advanced Guided Practice

Exercise 4

Use the steps below to write the answers to the questions.

> **Step 1:** Read the questions (9 and 10 on the next page).
> **Step 2:** Read the passage once to understand the main idea. Underline important details.
> **Step 3:** Reread only what will help you answer questions.
> **Step 4:** Write the answer in your own words.
>   a. Restate the question.
>   b. Add specific information from the passage.
>   c. State your own thoughts if you think it will help you to explain your answer.

Opportunity Cost

Let's say that you have $2.00 to spend in a candy store. That seems pretty good, right? Then, you go into the candy store, and you see about $10.00 worth of candy that you would like to buy. You cannot have every piece of candy that you want. You have to make choices. If you choose one type of candy, then that means that you have to give up choosing another type of candy.

Every now and then, you must make choices about how you spend your money. What makes choosing difficult is that whenever you choose one thing, you give up something else. Governments face the same dilemma like the one that you might face in a candy store. People want things, but their governments are limited in what they can provide. Most decisions that governments make will leave some people feeling unsatisfied.

When you, as an individual, or a government, as a whole, make a choice about how to spend money, there is usually something else that is sacrificed. When you choose to buy a chocolate bar, you give up the opportunity to buy sour candy. When a government chooses to build a new bridge, the government may give up the opportunity to build a new library. There is a name for this type of sacrifice: opportunity cost. Opportunity cost is the cost of what you give up whenever you make a choice.

Although opportunity cost is often thought of in terms of money, there are opportunity costs associated with every resource. For example, the opportunity cost of watching a 30 minute television program might be that you give up the opportunity to spend those 30 minutes playing a video game, finishing your homework, or baking cookies.

Although it's hard to measure opportunity cost, it is a very real thing. For example, if you spend time watching TV, it's hard to measure the cost of giving up the other things that you could have done with your time. However, it is a real cost nevertheless. Also, people tend not to think about opportunity cost very much. Why would you think about having given up sour candy when you're eating a delicious chocolate bar? And why would you think about having given up the opportunity to play a video game when you're enjoying a great TV program? Even though opportunity cost is hard to measure, and often is hidden, it is something to consider when making a tough decision.

9. Why might some people feel unsatisfied if their local government decides to build a new bridge? Explain your answer in terms of opportunity cost.

_____

_____

_____

_____

_____

_____

10. Let's say that the governor of your state decides to build a shopping mall in an empty field in the middle of your state. The governor tells you that, in building the shopping mall, there is nothing to lose. What would you tell the governor?

_____

_____

_____

_____

_____

_____

© 2013 The Critical Thinking Co.™ • www.CriticalThinking.com • 800-458-4849

There are many good answers to the questions about opportunity cost.

Below are examples of how Sophia and some other kids answered the questions.

The answers that you gave will probably not be exactly like the answers below, and that's okay.

If you have **restated the question** and have used **specific information from the passage** in your answer, then you have given a good answer.

9. Why might some people feel unsatisfied if their local government decides to build a new bridge? Explain your answer in terms of opportunity cost.

If a government decides to build a new bridge, some people might be unsatisfied because the government is giving up the opportunity to do something else instead of building the new bridge.

Some people might feel unsatisfied if their local government decides to build a new bridge. They might feel this way because their government is giving up the opportunity to do something else with the money that is being used to build the bridge. Some people might feel unsatisfied because they want a new library and not a new bridge.

10. Let's say that the governor of your state decides to build a shopping mall in an empty field in the middle of your state. The governor tells you that, in building the shopping mall, there is nothing to lose. What would you tell the governor?

I would tell the governor that he really does have something to lose. If he builds the shopping mall, then he gives up the opportunity for that field to be a playground, or a school, or something else. The shopping mall is not a bad idea, but it is important that the governor think about other things that could be done with the land.

I would remind the governor about hidden opportunity costs by telling him about what he would be giving up if he chose to build the shopping mall. If he builds the shopping mall, then he gives up the opportunity to build something else, like a bridge or a park.

V. Use Clues to Infer Answers

When you answer questions about what you have read on a test, many times you will find the answers directly in the passage. So far, that's what you've been practicing in this book.

However, there are times you will **not** find answers directly in the passage. Instead, you will have to infer the answers. To infer is to draw your own conclusions from clues in the passage in order to answer the questions.

This exercise will show you the difference between finding answers directly in the passage and inferring answers by using clues.

Step 1: Read the questions (1 and 2 that are below the passage).

Step 2: Read the passage once to understand the main idea. Underline important details.

Exercise 1

Women in Space

In 1961, an astronaut from Russia named Yuri Gagarin was the first person to travel in outer space. People around the world were amazed when they learned that a person traveled in outer space. One ten year old girl from America who heard this news was Sally Ride. This news made Sally wish that she could become an astronaut one day. Just as space travel is amazing, it also is amazing when children grow up to accomplish their dreams.

Step 3: Reread the underlined details to help you answer the questions.

1. Write the year that the first person traveled in outer space. _____

To answer question 1, you can look at the passage and find the answer directly. You may already have underlined the answer. The correct answer is 1961.

2. What did Sally Ride probably do when she grew up?

_____

a. Restate the question.
b. Then add specific information from the passage.

© 2013 The Critical Thinking Co.™ • www.CriticalThinking.com • 800-458-4849

To answer question 2, you cannot find the answer directly in the passage. You need to **infer** the answer using **clues** from the passage.

There are three clues in the passage. Here's how to use those clues to infer the answer:

Clue: "This news made Sally wish that she could become an astronaut one day."

Inference: When Sally was a child, she wanted to become an astronaut.

Clue: "Just as space travel is amazing, it also is amazing when children grow up to accomplish their dreams."

Inference: Sally may have grown up to become an astronaut.

Clue: Look at the **photo** next to the passage.

Inference: The woman in the photo is dressed like a NASA astronaut. Maybe that's Sally Ride.

Using clues from the passage, you can infer the answer. The best answer is:

When Sally Ride grew up, she probably became an astronaut.

Some kids are nervous when they need to infer answers. Here's what one student (Scott) said about inferring answers:

"I make inferences about what will happen when I read for fun. Now when I take a test I know I can use clues from the passage to infer the best answer."

To answer some questions, you **must** infer answers because you may not find those answers directly in the passage. To infer, you need to find clues, put those clues together, and decide on the best answer.

Guided Practice

Follow the steps below to practice making inferences.

> **Step 1:** Read the questions (3, 4, and 5 on the next page).
> **Step 2:** Read the passage once to understand the main idea. Underline important details.
> **Step 3:** Reread the underlined details to help you answer the questions.

Exercise 2

Kwan's Birthday Wish

The candles on Kwan's birthday cake were lit. Kwan knew that he would have to make a wish soon. He thought that he might wish for a new video game. However, he really did not want a new video game. He wondered if there was something else that could be his wish. To help him think of another wish that might be better than a video game, he said to his guests, "Help me out by telling me things that you want for your birthdays."

Kwan's mother said, "That is very kind of you, but it is your birthday, and your wish."

"Yeah mom," explained Kwan, "it's my wish, but I'm not sure what to wish, and if I hear more choices, maybe then I can make a really good wish."

Kwan's friend Jason said, "You should wish for a longer lunch time in school because you never finish your lunch."

Kwan laughed and said, "Is that what you would wish for on your birthday Jason?"

"No," answered Jason, "I would wish for a kitten."

"But I already have a cat!" exclaimed Kwan, who was looking at the candles burning and losing his patience.

Abe, another friend from school suggested, "Just wish for a super power, like being able to fly."

"No way," argued Kwan. "Even though I'm not happy with the wish I'm thinking of, at least it's a wish that can come true," and blew out his candles before it was too late.

                        © 2013 The Critical Thinking Co.™ • www.CriticalThinking.com • 800-458-4849

3. What did Kwan's mother probably think that Kwan was going to do when he asked, "Help me out by telling me things that you want for your birthdays."
    a. She thought that Kwan would give his birthday wish to someone else.
    b. She thought that Kwan would wish for a video game.
    c. She thought that Kwan would wish for a kitten.
    d. She thought that Kwan didn't want to make a wish.

Cross out wrong answers, and then choose the best answer.

Clue: "Kwan's mother said, 'That is very kind of you, but it is your birthday, and your wish.' "

4. Why did Kwan ask to hear other kids' wishes?
    a. Because he didn't have any wishes of his own.
    b. Because he did not like his own wish, and he thought that someone else's wish would be something that he would want for himself.
    c. Because he wanted to know if other kids also wanted a video game.
    d. Because it was not really his birthday.

Clue: "He thought that he might wish for a new video game. However, he really did not want a new video game. He wondered if there was something else that could be his wish. To help him think of another wish that might be better than a video game, he said to his guests, 'Help me out by telling me things that you want for your birthdays.' "

5. In the end, just before he blew out the candles, what was probably Kwan's wish?
    a. a kitten
    b. a super power
    c. a video game
    d. the ability to fly

Clue: "He thought that he might wish for a new video game. However, he really did not want a new video game. He wondered if there was something else that could be his wish."

Clue: " 'But I already have a cat!' said Kwan, who was looking at the candles burning and losing his patience."

Clue: "' No way,' said Kwan. 'Even though I'm not happy with the wish I'm thinking of, at least it's a wish that can come true,' and blew out his candles before it was too late."

Try to do the following exercises without looking at the steps. (Remember to look at the questions on the next page before you read the passage.)

Exercise 3

Poison Sumac

Laura and Sylvia were out at recess when Laura noticed a small bush with big, bright, red flowers. Laura knew that her teacher, Ms. Fermi, loved the color red. Laura told Sylvia, "I have a perfect idea about how we can surprise Ms. Fermi." Laura grabbed Sylvia's hand and walked with Sylvia toward the bush.

As they got close to the bush, they heard the playground monitor shout, "Stay away from that bush." Sylvia dropped Laura's hand and walked away, but Laura waited for the playground monitor to move out of sight, and then she picked the flowers off of the bush.

After recess, Laura walked proudly into the classroom and placed the flowers on Ms. Fermi's desk. Laura returned to her seat and imagined Ms. Fermi exclaiming that she loved the flowers, and then imagined Ms. Fermi begging to know which thoughtful student placed the flowers on her desk. Instead, when Ms. Fermi walked into the classroom and saw the flowers, she immediately picked up the phone and said, "I need a custodian to come dispose of poison sumac flowers."

Laura sat very still at her desk and put her hand over her mouth. She didn't know what to say or do next. Should she tell Ms. Fermi that she picked the poison sumac flowers? Just then, the custodian came through the doorway, picked up the flowers, and announced, "It's sumac all right, but it's not poison sumac. It's called Staghorn Sumac, and it's not poisonous at all."

Clues are provided for questions 6-8 below.

6. In the playground, Sylvia dropped Laura's hand and walked away because:
   a. Sylvia didn't like the flowers.
   b. Sylvia knew that the flowers were poisonous.
   c. Sylvia did not want to be Laura's friend.
   d. Sylvia obeyed the playground monitor.

Clue: "As they got close to the bush, they heard the playground monitor shout, 'Stay away from that bush.' Sylvia dropped Laura's hand and walked away, but Laura waited for the playground monitor to move out of sight, and then she picked the flowers off of the bush."

7. How did Laura feel **right after** she walked into the classroom and placed the flowers on Ms. Fermi's desk?
   a. frightened, because the playground monitor had told her to stay away from the flowers
   b. frightened, because she thought that Ms. Fermi might be poisoned by the flowers
   c. proud, because she was the first student to go back into the classroom after recess
   d. proud, because she thought that Ms. Fermi would love the flowers

Clue: "Laura returned to her seat and imagined Ms. Fermi exclaiming that she loved the flowers, and then imagined Ms. Fermi begging to know which thoughtful student placed the flowers on her desk."

8. When Laura sat very still at her desk and put her hand over her mouth, she was probably worried that:
   a. she might have been poisoned by the flowers.
   b. she had disappointed her friend Sylvia.
   c. the flowers did not look beautiful.
   d. Ms. Fermi would touch the flowers and be poisoned.

Clue: "Instead, when Ms. Fermi walked into the classroom and saw the flowers, she immediately picked up the phone and said, 'I need a custodian to come dispose of poison sumac flowers.'"

"Laura sat very still at her desk and put her hand over her mouth. She didn't know what to say or do next. Should she tell Ms. Fermi that she picked the poison sumac flowers?"

© 2013 The Critical Thinking Co.™ • www.CriticalThinking.com • 800-458-4849

Exercise 4

Red Lizard

One evening in the desert, a red lizard climbed onto a high rock to catch flies for his dinner. It was just before sunset. Darkness would soon come to the desert. After dark, the flies would settle down for the night.

As the red lizard climbed onto the high rock, he saw that a yellow lizard was already on the rock. The yellow lizard was standing very still, waiting to catch flies for his dinner, too. After some time, a swarm of tiny dust flies passed by the high rock. The yellow lizard gobbled the tiny flies with gusto, saying that they were delicious. The red lizard frowned upon the yellow lizard and bragged, "I am too grand a lizard to eat such tiny flies."

After the swarm of tiny dust flies moved past the high rock, the yellow lizard, feeling full and happy, said goodbye to the red lizard. The yellow lizard climbed down from the rock for a good night's sleep. But the red lizard stood alone and waited. As the red lizard waited, very still, he felt that a huge, juicy fly would come his way soon. But none came. Then, the sun set. No more flies, huge or tiny, would come. The red lizard climbed down from the high rock in the darkness. He muttered sadly to himself, "I was too picky."

© 2013 The Critical Thinking Co.™ • www.CriticalThinking.com • 800-458-4849

9. Which sentence about the red lizard is **most likely** true?
   a. He is friends with the yellow lizard.
   b. He thinks that he is too good to eat tiny flies.
   c. He enjoys eating all kinds of food.
   d. He does not like being red.

10. Write the sentence in the passage that gave you the best clue to the answer to question 9.

_____

_____

11. If the red lizard learns from his mistake, then the next time that he climbs the high rock, he most likely will:
   a. eat whatever flies come his way.
   b. wait for a huge, juicy fly again.
   c. be kind to the yellow lizard.
   d. go to a rock that he does not have to share with the yellow lizard.

12. Write the sentence in the passage that gave you the best clue to the answer to question 11.

_____

_____

13. What is the meaning of the word <u>gusto</u> in this sentence:
   "The yellow lizard gobbled the tiny flies with <u>gusto</u>, saying that they were delicious."
   a. embarrassment
   b. sadness
   c. enjoyment
   d. slowness

> When you take a test, you will often be asked about the meaning of words. Use the steps that you have already learned (Section I) in order to figure out what the vocabulary word <u>gusto</u> means.
> **Step 1:** Think about what the word means before you look at the answer choices.
> **Step 2:** Try each answer choice in the sentence.
> **Step 3:** Cross out answers that do not make sense, and then choose the best answer.

Exercise 5

Block City
(adapted from a poem by Robert Louis Stevenson)

What are you able to build with your blocks?
You can build castles and palaces, ships and docks.
Rain may keep raining, and others may roam,
But you can be happy and building at home.

Let the sofa be mountains, the carpet be sea,
There you can build a city for me.
A store and a castle and a palace beside,
And a harbor as well where my ships may ride.

As I used to see it, I see it again,
The castles and kings and ships and men,
And as long as I live and wherever I may be,
I will always remember my city by the sea.

14. What happens in this poem?
   a. An adult sees a child building with blocks, and then remembers building a block city when he was a child.
   b. Two children argue about what they should play together.
   c. A boy decides to save his money so that he can buy a big set of blocks.
   d. A younger child knocks down an older child's block city.

15. Reread the last four lines of the poem. How do those last four lines of the poem help you to figure out the answer to question 14?

_____

_____

_____

_____

Congratulations! You have learned how to do your best when you use clues to infer answers.
Check your answers in the Answer Key on page 215.

If you would like to practice with more difficult questions, you can go on to the Advanced Guided Practice. However, if you would like to stop here, that is fine.

© 2013 The Critical Thinking Co.™ • www.CriticalThinking.com • 800-458-4849

Advanced Guided Practice

Use the steps below to answer the questions.

> **Step 1:** Read the questions (on the next page).
> **Step 2:** Read the passage once to understand the main idea. Underline important details.
> **Step 3:** Reread the underlined details to help you answer the questions.

Exercise 6

My Shark Presentation
by Jasmine Diller

Sharks are the most interesting creatures in the animal kingdom. So, when it was time to choose a topic for my class presentation, it was easy. Ms. Hernandez said that we could choose any topic that we found extremely interesting. For me, that topic is sharks.

Sharks are cool because they swim very fast and swim almost constantly. They keep moving so that water can pass over their gills. The water passing over their gills is what allows them to breathe. So, sharks move a lot, and they tend to move very fast. Their speed is what makes them so cool.

To prepare for my class presentation, I had to do research. I had to find out some facts about sharks. I thought I knew a lot about sharks, but there were a few things I didn't know. For example, I found out that there are 354 different species of sharks. I didn't know that there were that many different kinds of sharks. I also found out that even though most sharks are kind of big, some are small, and the smallest kind of shark is the dwarf lanternshark. The dwarf lanternshark is only a few inches long, so it is small enough to live in a fish tank. I also found out that not all sharks are carnivores, and there are many that eat only plants.

I wrote each of these facts on index cards, just as Ms. Hernandez said we should. After Ms. Hernandez checked our index cards, she announced to the class that we should now find pictures, charts, or any images that would help us present our topic to the class. I thought this part of the project was great, because I love looking for images on the Internet. I found the coolest pictures to show the class, and I had an image that matched what I had to say on each of my index cards.

I thought that I was ready for my presentation. But then, presentation day came. I felt a knot in my stomach as the first students gave their presentations. I heard my classmate, Anna, give her presentation right before it was going to be my turn. Anna's presentation seemed to be interesting to the rest of the class, but I was not able to comprehend anything that she said.

When Anna finished, I clutched my index cards and images and walked to the front of the classroom on weak, wobbly legs. When I faced the class, I felt as though I could not speak. Then I looked at the first index card. I tried to read it out loud, but I don't know if what I said were the words on the index card or something altogether different. Just then, I saw Anna, who was sitting right in front of me, give me the "thumbs up." I looked up a little more and saw Ms. Hernandez nodding, as if she liked what I said.

© 2013 The Critical Thinking Co.™ • www.CriticalThinking.com • 800-458-4849

As I held up my image that showed the diversity of sharks, I pointed out that most sharks are very big. But I also pointed out that there are some sharks that are so small that they can live in a fish tank. Without having planned it, I said, "I want to get the smallest type of shark, a dwarf lanternshark, which is only a few inches long, for the fish tank in my living room so that I can tell everyone that there's a shark in my home." The class laughed!

I continued my presentation, covering all the information on my index cards, and showing all my images. When I finished, I walked to my seat in the back of the classroom on legs that felt a little stronger. The class applauded! I sat down, smiling and exhaling deeply, feeling unexpectedly confident. Although presenting the project in front of the class was scary at first, I learned a lot from doing something that was very difficult for me.

16. Who, most likely, is Ms. Hernandez? List two specific clues from the passage that led you to your answer.

   _____

   _____

   _____

   _____

17. The **most important** lesson that Jasmine learned from having given her shark presentation was probably that:
   a. she had a good sense of humor and could make people laugh.
   b. she could actually keep her very own shark as a pet.
   c. Ms. Hernandez was supportive and kind.
   d. confidence comes when you do something difficult.

18. Which of these facts did Jasmine probably already know about sharks before she did research for her presentation?
   a. There are 354 different species of sharks.
   b. Some sharks are very small.
   c. Sharks breathe by passing water over their gills.
   d. Not all sharks are carnivores.

19. When Jasmine held up the image that showed the diversity of sharks, what did the class most likely see?
   a. a diagram of a shark's body
   b. a diagram showing many different kinds of sharks
   c. a photo of a real shark swimming in the ocean
   d. a chart showing the various foods that sharks eat

                    © 2013 The Critical Thinking Co.™ • www.CriticalThinking.com • 800-458-4849

20. What part of the project did Jasmine probably think was the most fun?
    a. choosing the topic
    b. writing down facts about the topic on index cards
    c. finding images to present to the class
    d. presenting the project in front of the class

21. Write the sentence(s) from the passage that gives the best clue(s) to the correct answer to question 20.

_____

_____

_____

_____

22. Which of these adjectives best describes Jasmine as she was listening to Anna's presentation?
    a. bored
    b. interested
    c. nervous
    d. excited

23. How do you think Jasmine will feel the next time she gives a class presentation? Use a detail from the passage to support your answer.

_____

_____

_____

_____

Exercise 7

Invisible Sister

To our mom, she's a lovely, floating hat.
To her baseball coach, she's a magical swinging bat.
To her teacher, she's a voice who knows "all that."
But to me, her big brother, she's just a pesky little gnat.

Doctors say she's a wonder,
Nature made a miraculous blunder.
An invisible girl is new to our world,
But with me,
We just sit and watch TV.

I know her power is beyond measure,
And she's called a "national treasure."
But my only wish
Is that we play a game of "Go Fish."
And it wouldn't hurt
If she stopped stealing my dessert.

24. Which of these statements would the invisible girl's teacher probably agree with?
    a. The invisible girl is a good student.
    b. The invisible girl watches too much TV.
    c. The invisible girl plays tricks on other students.
    d. The invisible girl is often late to school.

25. What is an example of the narrator's invisible sister being a "pesky little gnat"?
    a. She sits and watches TV with him.
    b. She plays baseball on a team.
    c. She steals his dessert.
    d. She plays a game of "Go Fish" with him.

26. How does the narrator seem to feel about having an invisible sister?
    a. He feels that she is a national treasure.
    b. He feels that she pretends to know things that she does not really know.
    c. He feels upset that he is not the one in the family who is invisible.
    d. He feels that she is an ordinary sister, even though she is also invisible.

© 2013 The Critical Thinking Co.™ • www.CriticalThinking.com • 800-458-4849

VI. Use Your Thoughts ~~and Feelings~~
to Infer Answers

You have already learned how to infer answers by using clues from a passage. It is not always easy to find clues. Sometimes, the best clue does <u>not</u> come from the passage. The <u>best</u> clue may come from *your own thoughts ~~and feelings~~* about a passage.

"I used to think that I could not pay attention to my own thoughts and feelings when I read something on a test. I thought that the only thing I should pay attention to is the passage and what it says.

Now I know that I should pay attention to how I feel and what I think when I read a passage. Sometimes, my own thoughts and feelings give me the most important information about the passage."

Here are four types of questions where you will have to use your own thoughts and feelings to figure out the answers:

1. Author's Purpose

> If you are asked why an author wrote a passage, it is up to you to decide the **author's purpose**, or reason for writing.

2. Tone and Mood

> If you are asked how the author feels about something or how the passage makes you feel, you will need to use your own feelings to infer the **tone and mood** of the passage.

3. Fact or Opinion?

> If you are asked whether a statement is a **fact** or an **opinion**, you will have to decide whether the statement can be proven or not.

4. Figurative Language

> If you are asked to infer the meaning and purpose of **figurative language** in the passage, you will have to rely on your own thoughts and feelings.

1. Author's Purpose

Whenever someone writes something, there is a reason. Authors always have a reason, or purpose, for writing.

There are many reasons why authors write. Below are the three main reasons:

a. **To inform** readers about facts, news, and things that may be useful

> Passages that inform are often called **articles**. You can find articles in newspapers, magazines, books, and online that teach you things like science and math. Articles that inform are usually nonfiction. But sometimes, fiction can inform readers too.

b. **To tell a story** that shares an experience or entertains readers

> Most of the reading that you do for fun was written by an author who wanted to tell a **story**. A story about something that happened to the author is sometimes called a **personal narrative**. A story can also be about something that really happened to someone else (nonfiction), or it can be about something that is made up (fiction).

c. **To convince** readers to do something or to change their opinions

> Authors can convince readers to do things like take care of the environment or be respectful of people who are different from themselves. Also, almost all **advertisements** are written to convince people to buy things.

> "Can an author have **more than one purpose**?"

> Yes! Some of the best advertisements are ones that entertain you and also inform you about some facts you may not have known. Also, some of the best, most entertaining stories can teach you lessons and convince you to try new things.

© 2013 The Critical Thinking Co.™ • www.CriticalThinking.com • 800-458-4849

The following passages cover different types of authors' purposes. Use the steps below to choose the answer that best describes the author's purpose for writing the passage.

Step 1: Read the question (below the passage).
Step 2: Read the passage ONCE to understand the main idea. Underline important details.
Step 3: Reread the underlined details to help you answer the question.

Exercise 1

My Fishy Morning

I woke up in my bowl this morning, stretched my fins, and swam over to my plant. It looked the same as it had every other day, but I looked it over thoroughly just the same. You never know when a new leaf or branch may decide to start growing. After looking it over, I did my customary swim of two times around the entire plant.

After my customary swim around the plant, I decided to do something different. I looked around for a while, and then I darted down to the bottom of my bowl to look at the pebbles. Impulsively, I picked up a small pebble with my mouth, and then, "Patooeh!" I spat it out. It shot across my bowl in a powerful burst. Feeling proud, I looked at my reflection on the side of the bowl. What a fine fish I am!

1. The author's main purpose for writing *My Fishy Morning* was to:
    a. inform readers about what fish do inside their bowls.
    b. entertain readers with a story about what a fish might be thinking.
    c. convince readers that the fish in the story is a fine fish.

Remember: Cross out wrong answers, and then choose the best answer.

© 2013 The Critical Thinking Co.™ • www.CriticalThinking.com • 800-458-4849

Exercise 2

Grip Strength

During a football game, football players must be able to catch and hold on to the football. The ability to hold on to the football is called grip strength. In order to improve their grip strength, some football players put tape around their fingers. They think that the tape will make their fingers less slippery and improve their grip on the ball. If you see a football game on TV or in person, you might see some players with tape around their fingers. Now you know that they use the tape on their fingers in order to improve their grip strength.

> Remember, even if you don't understand every detail, you should be able to understand the main idea.

2. The author's main purpose for writing *Grip Strength* was to:
    a. inform readers about the reason some football players wear tape on their fingers.
    b. tell a story about football players putting tape around their fingers.
    c. convince football players to tape their fingers.

Exercise 3

Bubblegood

Bubblegood is the best toothpaste you can buy. Also, it tastes like bubblegum! Of course, brushing your teeth is a big part of dental health because it fights cavities and keeps your gums healthy. Did you know that brushing with Bubblegood toothpaste keeps you brushing longer because it tastes so good? When you brush longer, it helps your teeth and gums stay healthier. Go out and buy Bubblegood toothpaste today!

3. The author's main purpose for writing *Bubblegood* was to:
    a. inform readers about dental health.
    b. entertain readers with a story about why you should brush your teeth.
    c. convince readers to buy Bubblegood toothpaste.

> **Did you notice** that finding the author's purpose is a lot like finding the main idea? That's because author's purpose, or reason for writing, is usually the **same** as the main idea.

© 2013 The Critical Thinking Co.™ • www.CriticalThinking.com • 800-458-4849

Exercise 4

Your Own Little Army

When you think of bacteria, you probably think of germs, which can make you sick. However, did you know that some types of bacteria are good for you? There are good bacteria that live on your skin and help you by fighting off bad bacteria that can make you sick. You can think of these good bacteria as your own little army.

Your own little army works hard to protect you. If they see bad bacteria, they send out a battle cry, shouting, "Come on, let's get the bad guys!" Then they march into battle. They surround the bad bacteria and eat them up! When this happens, your army has done its job and has protected you.

Your army of good bacteria does its job very well. You have a job, too. Your job is to eat healthy foods and get plenty of sleep. When you stay healthy, your army of good bacteria is strong. So, do your job and stay healthy, and your army of good bacteria will stay strong and do its job, too!

4. The author's main purpose for writing the **first paragraph** of *Your Own Little Army* was to:
   a. inform you about the good bacteria that live on your skin by describing them as your own little army.
   b. entertain you with a story of how good bacteria act like your own little army.
   c. convince you to eat healthy food and go to bed on time so that you can help your own little army.

5. The author's main purpose for writing the **second paragraph** of *Your Own Little Army* was to:
   a. inform you about the good bacteria that live on your skin by describing them as your own little army.
   b. entertain you with a story of how good bacteria act like your own little army.
   c. convince you to eat healthy food and go to bed on time so that you can help your own little army.

6. The author's main purpose for writing the **third paragraph** of *Your Own Little Army* was to:
   a. inform you about the good bacteria that live on your skin by describing them as your own little army.
   b. entertain you with a story of how good bacteria act like your own little army.
   c. convince you to eat healthy food and go to bed on time so that you can help your own little army.

© 2013 The Critical Thinking Co.™ • www.CriticalThinking.com • 800-458-4849

2. Tone and Mood

The **tone** of a passage is the feeling that the **author** or a character seem to have about the passage. The **mood** of a passage is the feeling that **you** get when you read the passage.

For example, here's a sentence that begins a passage:

> After sunset, the forest suddenly turned darker than the night sky, and the leaves on the forest floor began to spin in the wild, wicked wind.

Here are some words that students wrote to describe the **tone** and **mood** of the sentence:

"scary"

"wicked"

"creepy"

"The forest is haunted."

"Something bad will happen."

The passage that begins with that sentence is actually a **scary story**. Often in a scary story, even before anything happens, you get a feeling that something scary might happen.

The author is creating a **scary tone**. Nothing really scary has happened yet. However, when you read about a dark forest with leaves spinning in the wild, wicked wind, you can infer that the **tone** is scary, and that something scary might happen.

© 2013 The Critical Thinking Co.™ • www.CriticalThinking.com • 800-458-4849

Read each passage, and write one or two words that describe the tone of each passage in the space provided.

Exercise 5

I asked my dad to take me to Junior's Toy Store because I had saved my allowance to buy a remote controlled airplane. Junior's is a long way from our home, but I wanted to go there instead of any other store because they were having a sale. When we finally arrived, they didn't have any airplanes left!

7. Write one or two words that describe how the **person telling the passage** might feel. (tone)

_____

_____

Exercise 6

I shifted the weight of my body from one foot to the other as I stood in line to ride the roller coaster. I took a few deep breaths as I saw the next group of people climb inside the roller coaster cars. Even though I had waited a long time in line, I was starting to wonder whether or not it was a good idea to ride the roller coaster.

8. Write one or two words that describe how the **person telling the passage** might feel. (tone)

_____

_____

Read each passage, and write one or two words that describe the mood of each passage in the space provided.

Exercise 7

Selena, the goddess of the moon, comes out at night to light up the world. She rides her silver horse across the night sky, sprinkling stardust upon the sleeping Earth.

9. Write one or two words that describe how the passage makes **you** feel. (mood)

_____

_____

Exercise 8

Down in the depths of a sand castle by the sea,
None other than a crab was staring up at me.
Scurry away? Oh no, not he.
This was his castle, not mine, you see.

"Who are you?" he said. "Are you going to flee?"
"Please don't" he said. "Come and join me for tea!"
"But you're a crab!" I said, and looked for someone to come see
This talking little crab who wanted to have tea!

10. Write one or two words that describe how the poem makes **you** feel. (mood)

_____

_____

© 2013 The Critical Thinking Co.™ • www.CriticalThinking.com • 800-458-4849

3. Fact or Opinion?

Sometimes, you will have to decide whether a statement in a passage is a **fact** or an **opinion**.

A fact is something that you can prove.
An opinion is someone's feeling or thought about something. There is no way to prove an opinion. You cannot see any proof of a person's feelings or thoughts.

When you need to decide whether a statement is a fact or an opinion, ask yourself:

Can I see proof?

If you can see proof, then the statement is probably a fact. If there is no proof, then the statement is probably an opinion.

Read this statement:

Apples taste better than oranges.

Can you see any proof that apples taste better than oranges? No. This statement is someone's **feeling** or **thought**. In other words, it is an **opinion**. It is not a fact.

Now read this statement:

In a taste test, 82% of students at King Elementary School said that apples tasted better than oranges.

Here, the author is showing you proof. A taste test and the result of a taste test is a real thing that you can see. This statement is not someone's thought or feeling. It is a **fact**.

Read this statement:

> Most students at King Elementary School <u>say</u> that apples taste better than oranges.

This statement is about something that students **say**. You can see and hear students when they say things. If you can see and hear something, then you can get proof that it is a **fact**.

Now read this statement:

> Most students at King Elementary School <u>think</u> that apples taste better than oranges.

This statement is exactly like the statement above, except the word <u>say</u> is replaced with the word <u>think</u>.

This statement is an **opinion** because it is not about anything that can be seen or proven. Instead, it is about a thought.

Clues that a statement is an opinion are the words "think," "feel," and "hope." You really cannot see or prove thoughts, feelings, or hopes.

You cannot see a thought, a feeling, or a hope. Those words express opinions.

Telling the difference between facts and opinions can get very tricky! Look at the last statement you read. That statement was an opinion. Yet, what is tricky is that the same statement can also be a fact if there is some proof:

> In a taste test, 82% of students at King Elementary School said that apples tasted better than oranges. Most students at King Elementary School think that apples taste better than oranges.

The second sentence is the same sentence that we had decided was an opinion. However, now that same sentence is **fact**. It is now a fact because **the sentence before it shows you proof**.

© 2013 The Critical Thinking Co.™ • www.CriticalThinking.com • 800-458-4849

Read the passage and answer questions about facts and opinions. Use the steps you learned when you read and answer the questions.

Step 1: Read the questions (11 and 12 on the next page).
Step 2: Read the passage once to understand the main idea. Underline important details.
Step 3: Reread only what will help you answer questions.
Step 4: Cross out the wrong answers, and then choose the best answer.

Exercise 9

A Field Trip to a Bread Factory Is Better Than a Field Trip to a Zoo

For our field trip, our class must choose between going to a bread factory or going to a zoo. I think that a trip to a bread factory is the better choice. I have four reasons why a trip to a bread factory is better than a trip to a zoo:

1. Our class has just learned about how products are made on assembly lines. The bread factory can show us a great example of an assembly line.

2. A trip to the bread factory is more convenient than a trip to the zoo. The zoo is about 40 miles away, and we would have to take a bus to get there. However, the bread factory is only about five blocks away from our school, and we could walk there. Also, if the weather is bad, we would have a miserable day at the zoo. However, no matter how bad the weather is, it would not bother us if we were inside the bread factory.

3. I think that some students will be angry with me for saying this, but the zoo is kind of stinky. I love animals just as much as everyone else, but when a zoo is stinky, it's just awful, no matter how great the animals are. However, the bread factory smells delicious!

4. Finally, most kids have already visited the zoo but not the bread factory. When our class was asked, "Who has been to the zoo?" almost every hand was raised. But, when our class was asked, "Who has been to the bread factory?" only one student raised his hand.

The bread factory tour is a better field trip than a day at the zoo. The bread factory tour would show us an example of what we've learned in class, it would be a convenient trip, a good smelling trip, and a trip where the fewest number of students have already been. For these reasons, I think that a field trip to the bread factory is better than a field trip to the zoo.

11. Which statement was proven in the passage to be a **fact**?
    a. The bread factory can show us a great example of an assembly line.
    b. If the weather is bad, we would have a miserable day at the zoo.
    c. I think that some students will be angry with me for saying this, but the zoo is kind of stinky.
    d. Most kids have already visited the zoo, but not the bread factory.

12. Which **fact** best supports the author's opinion that a trip to the bread factory would be more convenient than a trip to the zoo?
    a. The zoo that we would visit is about 40 miles away from the school, but the bread factory is only five blocks away.
    b. If the weather is bad, we would have a miserable day at the zoo.
    c. Most kids have already visited the zoo, but not the bread factory.
    d. When asked, "Who has been to the bread factory?" only one student raised his hand.

13. Complete the chart for each statement from the passage.

Statement	Is it Fact or Opinion?	
A. Our class has just learned about how products are made on assembly lines.	○ fact	○ opinion
B. The bread factory can show us a great example of an assembly line.	○ fact	○ opinion
C. The bread factory is only about five blocks away from our school, and we could walk there.	○ fact	○ opinion
D. If the weather is bad, we would have a miserable day at the zoo.	○ fact	○ opinion
E. I think that some students will be angry with me for saying this, but the zoo is kind of stinky.	○ fact	○ opinion
F. The bread factory smells delicious!	○ fact	○ opinion
G. When our class was asked, "Who has been to the zoo?" almost every hand was raised.	○ fact	○ opinion

© 2013 The Critical Thinking Co.™ • www.CriticalThinking.com • 800-458-4849

4. Figurative Language

Figurative language is fun. You hear it a lot, and you probably use it yourself. Here is an example of figurative language being used to describe the weather:

> Today the weather has been <u>on a roller coaster ride</u>. This morning it was <u>as hot as blazes</u>. Then, suddenly, the air became much cooler, and it started <u>raining cats and dogs</u>.

Here is the same description of the weather, only this time, figurative language is <u>not</u> used:

> Today the weather has been changing a lot. This morning it was very hot. Then, suddenly, the air became much cooler, and it started raining heavily.

Which description do you like best? The first description, the one that used figurative language, was more fun to read. However, the second description, the one that did not use figurative language, was not as fun, but may have been easier to understand.

Sometimes figurative language is hard to understand. For example, have you ever seen cats and dogs fall from the sky? No, you have not! If you have never heard that figurative language before, you might have a hard time inferring that "raining cats and dogs" really means "raining heavily."

Here are three types of figurative language: **similes**, **metaphors**, and **idioms**.

a. Similes

A **simile** describes something by comparing it to something else using **like** or **as**. Here is a simile from the weather description:

> "This morning it was <u>as hot as blazes</u>."

Below are some other similes:

> After winning first prize, Henry felt <u>as proud as a peacock</u>.
> Gabby was <u>as quiet as a mouse</u> while the baby was sleeping.
> The twins were <u>like two peas in a pod</u>.

14. Fill in the blank spaces below to write a simile.

> She ran through the obstacle course as _____ as a _____.

b. Metaphors

A **metaphor** also describes something, but instead of comparing it to something else, a metaphor actually calls it something else.   Here is a metaphor from the weather description:

"Today the weather has been <u>on a roller coaster ride</u>."

Below are some other metaphors:

Her messy room was a <u>disaster area</u>.
The busy store was a <u>beehive of shoppers</u>.
All the different people in America make the country a <u>melting pot</u> of cultures.

15. Circle the sentence that uses a metaphor.
a. Mrs. Wiggins had a mountain of paper on her desk.
b. Mrs. Wiggins had so much paper on her desk that it was piled up like a mountain.
c. Mrs. Wiggins had a lot of paper on her desk.

c. Idioms

An **idiom** is an expression that says one thing, but means another.   Here is an idiom from the weather description:

"Then, suddenly, the air became much cooler, and it started <u>raining cats and dogs</u>."

Below are some other idioms that you may have heard, and their real meanings:

The noise was <u>driving me up a wall</u>. (The noise was annoying me.)
She was <u>on cloud nine</u>. (She was very happy.)
That fancy car <u>costs an arm and a leg</u>. (That fancy car is very expensive.)

16. Write an idiom you have heard recently.

_____

_____

_____

If you can't think of an idiom right now, within a few days you probably will hear one!

© 2013 The Critical Thinking Co.™ • www.CriticalThinking.com • 800-458-4849

When you take a test, your job is to infer the meanings of figures of speech. To do this, you can **use the same steps you used when you figured out the meanings of vocabulary words.**

Step 1: Think about what the word means before you look at the answer choices.
Step 2: Try each answer choice in the sentence.
Step 3: Cross out answer choices that do not make sense.
Step 4: Choose the best answer.

Choose the answer that means the same thing as the underlined figure of speech.

17. After a long day of hard work, Ms. Beasley put on her pajamas and hit the hay.
    a. fed the cows
    b. swatted the hay with a broom
    c. read a book
    d. went to sleep

18. When I watched the movie, I fell asleep because the movie was as dull as dishwater.
    a. gray and dirty
    b. very boring
    c. reminding me to wash the dishes
    d. about washing dishes

19. It is easy to see construction workers because they wear vests that are a loud color.
    a. horn-covered
    b. very bright
    c. noisy
    d. screaming

20. The brave fire fighter was like a rock during the emergency.
    a. not moving at all
    b. hard and cold
    c. strong and reliable
    d. a big boulder

© 2013 The Critical Thinking Co.™ • www.CriticalThinking.com • 800-458-4849

When you infer the meaning of a figure of speech, you also may need to infer **why** the author chose a particular figure of speech to express a thought.

For example, let's say that in a story a boy is having fun playing and falls into a puddle. If an author wants to describe the boy as "wet and slippery," but wants to make it seem fun, the best figurative language may be:

> The boy was as soaked and slippery as a wet <u>slide on a playground</u>.

However, let's say that the story is about a thief who falls into a puddle as he is running away from the police. If an author wants to describe the thief as "wet and slippery," the best figurative language may be:

> The thief was a <u>wet, slippery snake</u>.

When describing a boy who was having fun, he can be compared to a fun slide on a playground. Yet, when describing a thief, the thief can be compared to a snake, which is often considered to be a sneaky creature.

Choose the answer that best describes the meaning of the figure of speech.

21. One of the best athletes in the sport of boxing is a man named Mohammed Ali. When Mohammed Ali describes himself as a boxer, he says that he <u>floats like a butterfly, and stings like a bee</u>.

    The best reason a boxer would describe himself as a <u>butterfly</u> is because he:
    a. likes flowers.
    b. flies in the air.
    c. is delicate.
    d. is graceful and quick.

22. An advertisement for a mystery book describes the book as being <u>a fog of secrets</u>.

    The best reason a book would be described as <u>a fog of secrets</u> is because:
    a. it is very difficult to read, so it is kind of like a fog.
    b. it has a scary and mysterious tone, kind of like a fog.
    c. *Fog of Secrets* is the title of the book.
    d. the book is about foggy weather.

© 2013 The Critical Thinking Co.™ • www.CriticalThinking.com • 800-458-4849

VII. Understanding Analogies

An analogy shows two words that go together in a certain way. They have a relationship. You will often be asked on tests to find two other words that are related in the same way.

Here's an analogy:

Black and white are related in the same way as:
  a. color and rainbow.
  b. typewriter and newspaper.
  c. up and down.
  d. pencil and write.

Another way that an analogy can look is like this:

black : white ::
  a. color : rainbow
  b. typewriter : newspaper
  c. up : down
  d. pencil : write

Go ahead and choose the answer that you think has the same relationship as "black" and "white."

The correct answer is: up : down.

If you answered the question incorrectly, it's only because you haven't learned how to think carefully about analogies yet. You will practice skills that will help you solve analogies in this section.

Even if you chose the correct answer, you're going to feel much more confident about solving analogies after you practice the skills in this section.

Something that will help you solve any analogy is to <u>write a sentence *before* you look at the answer choices</u>. The sentence you write should describe how the two words in the question (like "black" and "white") are related.

Here's what happens when a student (Joss) writes a sentence to help him think about this analogy:

> black : white ::
>   a. color : rainbow
>   b. typewriter : newspaper
>   c. up : down
>   d. pencil : write

Joss thinks: "Before I look at the answer choices, I'm going to write a sentence that describes how 'black' and 'white' go together."

Joss writes: <u>Black is the opposite of white.</u>

Joss thinks: "Now I'm going to use that same sentence, but instead of 'black' and 'white,' I'm going to write 'is the opposite of' in all the answer choices."

a. color : rainbow	<u>Color is the opposite of rainbow.</u>
b. typewriter : newspaper	<u>Typewriter is the opposite of newspaper.</u>
c. up : down	<u>Up is the opposite of down.</u>
d. pencil : write	<u>Pencil is the opposite of write.</u>

Joss thinks: "<u>Up is the opposite of down</u> makes the most sense. The other sentences are not as good. So the right answer has to be up : down."

In the Guided Practice, you're going to practice exactly what Joss learned. First, you will see some sentences that describe relationships. Then, using those sentences, you will solve the analogies.

© 2013 The Critical Thinking Co.™ • www.CriticalThinking.com • 800-458-4849

Guided Practice

Choose the sentence that best describes the relationship between two words. Answers are provided on the next page.

1. Which sentence best describes how **tiny** and **small** go together?
    a. Tiny is the opposite of small.
    b. Tiny and small mean the same thing.
    c. Tiny is a part of something that is small.
    d. Tiny is a type of small.

2. Which sentence best describes how **scissors** and **cut** go together?
    a. Scissors are used to cut.
    b. Scissors cannot be used to cut.
    c. Scissors and cut mean the same thing.
    d. Scissors and cut are opposites.

3. Which sentence best describes how **July** and **summer** go together?
    a. July is the opposite of summer.
    b. July and summer mean the same thing.
    c. July is a month that is part of summer.
    d. July and summer are both months.

4. Which sentence best describes how **rose** and **flower** go together?
    a. A rose is the opposite of a flower.
    b. A rose and a flower are the same thing.
    c. A rose is a part of a flower.
    d. A rose is a type of flower.

5. Which sentence best describes how **kitten** and **cat** go together?
    a. A kitten grows up to be a cat.
    b. A kitten is the opposite of a cat.
    c. A kitten is the same as a cat.
    d. A kitten is part of a cat.

The correct sentences and the sentences Joss wrote for 1-5 are shown below. If you did not choose the correct sentence, it might be hard for you to solve the analogy.

Use the correct sentence and the sentences Joss wrote to help you solve each analogy. Circle the letter beside the correct answer.

1. tiny : small ::

   a. little : bug
   b. enormous : large
   c. big : smaller
   d. whale : huge

Tiny and small mean the same thing.

Little and bug mean the same thing.
Enormous and large mean the same thing.
Big and smaller mean the same thing.
Whale and huge mean the same thing.

2. scissors : cut ::

   a. hammer : tool
   b. pencil : write
   c. paper : pen
   d. knife : sharp

Scissors are used to cut.

A hammer is used to tool.
A pencil is used to write.
A paper is used to pen.
A knife is used to sharp.

3. July : summer ::

   a. January : cold
   b. October : Halloween
   c. North : South
   d. December : winter

July is a month that is part of summer.

January is a month that is part of cold.
October is a month that is part of Halloween.
North is a month that is part of South
December is a month that is part of winter.

4. rose : flower ::

   a. honey : bee
   b. grasshopper : insect
   c. egg : hatch
   d. shoe : foot

A rose is a type of flower.

Honey is a type of bee.
A grasshopper is a type of insect.
An egg is a type of hatch.
A shoe is a type of foot.

5. kitten : cat ::

   a. tiger : lion
   b. meow : roar
   c. pounce : run
   d. puppy : dog

A kitten grows up to be a cat.

A tiger grows up to be a lion.
A meow grows up to be a roar.
A pounce grows up to be a run.
A puppy grows up to be a dog.

© 2013 The Critical Thinking Co.™ • www.CriticalThinking.com • 800-458-4849

Did you know that there are five common analogies?

Common analogies are words that:

1. are <u>opposites</u> (also called *antonyms*) **black : white**
2. <u>mean the same thing</u> (also called *synonyms*) **tiny : small**
3. describe <u>how things are used</u> **scissors : cut**
4. describe a <u>part and a whole</u> (or whole and a part) **July : summer or summer : July**
5. describe a <u>type or an example</u> **rose : flower**

You should know about common analogies. However, there are many more types of analogies. For example, **kitten : cat** does not fit into any of the types listed above. **Kitten : cat** describes a different type of relationship altogether. <u>You always have to do your own careful thinking</u>.

Now you will practice writing your own sentences that describe the relationship between two words. Here's how to do it:

Write a sentence that tells someone (like a classmate) how the words are related. Explain the relationship as well as you can in just one sentence. If you get stuck, think about the common types of analogies that are described above.

In your sentence, always put the <u>first word first</u> and the <u>second word second</u>.

    cup : drink   A <u>cup</u> is used to <u>drink</u>.

6. Write a sentence that describes the relationship between **mittens** and **hands**.

_____

_____

7. Write a sentence that describes the relationship between **knee** and **leg**.

_____

_____

Below are examples of sentences that describe the relationships for 6 and 7. <u>These sentences are probably not exactly like the ones you wrote, and that is okay.</u> The important thing is that your sentences describe the relationships in a way that makes sense.

Use the sentences you wrote or the bold sentences below to help you solve each analogy. Circle the letter beside the correct answer.

6. mittens : hands ::
   a. hats : gloves
   b. umbrella : rain
   c. dogs : hamsters
   d. socks : feet

Mittens are worn on hands.
<u>Hats</u> are worn on <u>gloves.</u>
<u>Umbrellas</u> are worn on <u>rain.</u>
<u>Dogs</u> are worn on <u>hamsters.</u>
<u>Socks</u> are worn on <u>feet.</u>

You will notice something special about #7 below.

7. knee : leg ::
   a. heel : foot
   b. nose : face
   c. elbow : arm
   d. fingernail : finger

A knee is part of a leg.
A <u>heel</u> is part of a <u>foot</u>.
A <u>nose</u> is part of a <u>face</u>.
An <u>elbow</u> is part of an <u>arm</u>.
A <u>fingernail</u> is part of a <u>finger</u>.

"Hey, all of these sentences make sense!"

If all or none of your sentences make sense, go back and <u>write another sentence</u> to describe the relationship in the analogy. This time, <u>be more specific</u>. Write a little more about the relationship between the two words in the question.

Here's what happened when Joss wrote another sentence that was more specific:

7. knee : leg ::
   a. heel : foot
   b. nose : face
   c. elbow : arm
   d. fingernail : finger

A knee bends and is part of a leg.
A <u>heel</u> bends and is part of a <u>foot.</u>
A <u>nose</u> bends and is part of a <u>face.</u>
An <u>elbow</u> bends and is part of an <u>arm.</u>
A <u>fingernail</u> bends and is part of a <u>finger.</u>

Now you can see that only one of Joss's sentences (c) makes the most sense. So if your sentence doesn't work, try another one and be more specific.

Write a sentence that describes the relationship between the bold words. Later, you will use these sentences to help you solve analogies.

8. Write a sentence that describes the relationship between **Mars** and **planet**.

_____

_____

9. Write a sentence that describes the relationship between **snake** and **slithers**.

_____

_____

10. Write a sentence that describes the relationship between **stop** and **end**.

_____

_____

11. Write a sentence that describes the relationship between **electricity** and **light bulb**.

_____

_____

Below are examples of sentences that describe the relationships for 8-11. <u>These sentences are probably not exactly like the ones you wrote, and that is okay</u>. The important thing is that your sentences describe the relationships in a way that makes sense. Think about how each of the answer choices would fit in the sentence (see number 8 for Joss's sentences).

Use the sentences you wrote or the bold sentences below to help you solve each analogy. Circle the letter beside the correct answer.

8. Mars : planet ::
   a. moon : Earth
   b. Martian : Earthling
   c. North America : continent
   d. red : blue

Mars is a type of planet.
<u>Moon</u> is a type of <u>Earth</u>.
A <u>Martian</u> is a type of <u>Earthling</u>.
<u>North America</u> is a type of <u>continent</u>.
<u>Red</u> is a type of <u>blue</u>.

9. snake : slithers ::
   a. bird : egg
   b. rabbit : hops
   c. slide : slinks
   d. reptile : amphibian

A snake slithers so that it can move.

10. stop : end ::
    a. sign : red
    b. begin : end
    c. go : start
    d. high : low

Stop and end mean the same thing.

11. electricity : light bulb ::
    a. gas : car
    b. idea : bright
    c. Thomas Edison : invent
    d. power : glow

Electricity is needed to make a light bulb work.

     © 2013 The Critical Thinking Co.™ • www.CriticalThinking.com • 800-458-4849

Up until now, you have been **writing** a sentence that describes the analogy before you look at the answer choices.

Next you will **think** about a sentence that describes the analogy before you look at the answer choices.

Because you've practiced **writing** a sentence to describe an analogy, you will be much better at **thinking** about the analogy before you choose an answer. This kind of thinking will help you when you take a test.

Solve each of the analogies.

12. square : shape ::
    a. banana : fruit
    b. circle : triangle
    c. cube : sphere
    d. month : year

> **Think** of a sentence describing the analogy between "square" and "shape."

> **Think** about how each of the answer choices would fit in a sentence describing the analogy.

13. fish : fish tank ::
    a. dog : bone
    b. horse : horseshoe
    c. cow : barn
    d. guppy : fish food

14. dollar bill : paper ::
    a. money : rich
    b. quarter : penny
    c. car : metal
    d. president : Washington

15. racquet : tennis ::
    a. round : ball
    b. white : yellow
    c. bat : baseball
    d. socks : sneakers

16. frog : amphibian ::
    a. water : land
    b. eat : fly
    c. fish : lake
    d. dog : mammal

17. run : track ::
    a. seesaw : slide
    b. grass : sun
    c. play : playground
    d. dog : cat

© 2013 The Critical Thinking Co.™ • www.CriticalThinking.com • 800-458-4849

There are some analogies that give you **one word** of the answer, and your job is to find the **second word** of the answer. Even with this type of analogy, you should **think** about a sentence that describes the analogy before you look at the answer choices.

Circle the letter beside the correct answer.

18. poodle : dog :: chocolate : _____
    a. eat
    b. yummy
    c. flavor
    d. messy

> **Think** of a sentence describing the analogy between "poodle" and "dog."

> **Think** about how each of the answer choices would fit in a sentence describing the analogy.

19. ice : cold :: pillow : _____
    a. bed
    b. soft
    c. sleep
    d. hot

20. eat : apple :: drink : _____
    a. fruit
    b. strawberry
    c. straw
    d. water

Congratulations! You have learned how to do your best when you answer questions about analogies. Check your answers in the Answer Key on page 216.

If you would like to practice with more difficult questions, you can go on to the Advanced Guided Practice. However, if you would like to stop here, that is fine.

© 2013 The Critical Thinking Co.™ • www.CriticalThinking.com • 800-458-4849

Advanced Guided Practice

Solve each analogy.

21. always : never ::
     a. time : clock
     b. all : none
     c. once : twice
     d. some : sometimes

22. predict : future ::
     a. remember : past
     b. fortune : tell
     c. guess : chance
     d. time : pass

23. weight : scale ::
     a. length : ruler
     b. heavy : pound
     c. meter : centimeter
     d. distance : long

24. doctor : hospital ::
     a. book : library
     b. trumpet : band
     c. teacher : school
     d. tree : forest

25. baby : crawling ::
     a. cat : purring
     b. infant : crying
     c. fish : swimming
     d. bottle : eating

26. fake : real ::
     a. correct : right
     b. phone : phony
     c. plastic : paper
     d. false : true

27. rain : drop :: snow :
     a. freeze
     b. flake
     c. water
     d. fall

28. square : four :: pentagon : _____
     a. number
     b. shape
     c. five
     d. stop sign

29. two : second place :: one : _____
     a. finish
     b. one
     c. winner
     d. trophy

30. can : can't :: will : _____
     a. will not
     b. won't
     c. can't
     d. will

VIII. Estimate the Correct Answer

On tests, you will add, subtract, multiply, and divide numbers.

Even if you are good at math, you can make a mistake, especially when you work with big numbers that have a lot of **digits**. Everyone makes mistakes, but you can check your work by estimating the correct answer. When you estimate, you get an idea of what the correct answer should be.

Before you practice estimating the correct answer, you will first review **digits** and **place value**.

When you understand digits and place value, estimating the correct answer is very easy.

1. Understand Digits and Place Value
a. Digit*

A digit is a single, whole number from 0 – 9.

A big number, like 1,027, has four digits. The first digit is the number "1," the second digit is the number "0," the third digit is the number "2," and the fourth digit is the number "7."

1. Which of these numbers is **not** a digit?
    a. 3
    b. 15
    c. 1
    d. 2

2. How many digits are in the number 7,051?
    a. 2
    b. 7
    c. 4
    d. 0

3. Which of these numbers has 6 digits?
    a. 540,098
    b. 6
    c. 60,000
    d. 5,999

*In this book, "0" is called a digit. However, some teachers call "0" a "place holder" instead of a digit.

© 2013 The Critical Thinking Co.™ • www.CriticalThinking.com • 800-458-4849

b. Place Value

You probably have learned about **place value**.   Each digit in every number holds a place value.

Below is a Place Value Chart that shows the place value held by every digit in the number 3,829,146.

Place Value Chart

| millions | hundred thousands | ten thousands | thousands | hundreds | tens | ones |

If you were to say this number out loud, you would say:

"three million, eight hundred twenty-nine thousand, one hundred forty-six"

4. How many digits are in the number 3,829,146?
    a. 7
    b. 6
    c. 5
    d. 3 million

5. In the number 3,829,146, which digit is in the **ten thousands** place?
    a. 8
    b. 2
    c. 9
    d. 10

6. In the number 3,829,146, the digit "1" is in the:
    a. thousands place.
    b. hundreds place.
    c. tens place.
    d. ones place.

Check the Answer Key on page 217.

- If you correctly answered problems 1-6, then you understand digits and place value. You can go on to **How to Round Numbers**.

- If you answered more than one wrong, then you should review digits and place value with an adult before you go on to the rest of this chapter.

2. How to Round Numbers

Here's a problem that could be on a test. To estimate the correct answer, you must use **round numbers**. **Round numbers end in 0.** You can round to the nearest 10, or the nearest 100, or even the nearest 1,000.

$$428 + 973 \longrightarrow 400 + 1,000 = 1,400 \longrightarrow 428 + 973 = 1,401$$

Using round numbers makes estimating easy. It's easy to add 400 + 1,000. The answer will be close to 1,400.

To round numbers:

1. Underline the place value that you are rounding to. It can be the nearest 10, 100, or 1,000.

Usually, you will underline the **first digit** in the number. For example, if the number is 4,278, you will underline the 4, and round to the nearest 1,000. This way, you will work with only one digit, and the rest of them will be 0, which makes estimating easy. 4,278 = 4,000

2. Look one place to the right. If that number is 4 or less, the underlined number stays the same, and the rest of the numbers will be 0.   4,278 = 4,000

3. If that number is 5 or more, the underlined number goes up by one, and the rest of the numbers will be 0.   4,578 = 5,000

A way to remember this rule is to think "5 up." If the number is 5 or more, you round up.

Below is how a student (Ava) uses the steps to round the number 428 to the nearest 100.

428   First I underline the place I'm rounding to, which is the 100s place. 428

428   The 2 is one place to the right.
2 is less than 4, so the underlined number stays the same.
The round number is 400.

Now, here's what happens when Ava rounds 973 to the nearest 100.

973   First I underline the place I'm rounding to, which is the 100s place. 973

973   The 7 is one place to the right.
7 is more than 5, so the underlined number goes up one.
That means that the 9 changes to a 10. The round number is 1,000.

Finally, Ava uses the round numbers to estimate the answer:

$$428 + 973 \qquad 400 + 1,000 = 1,400$$

Now, I add the round numbers to estimate the answer.

I estimate that the answer is about 1,400.

© 2013 The Critical Thinking Co.™ • www.CriticalThinking.com • 800-458-4849

Guided Practice

Estimate each number to the nearest 10, and then estimate the total. Write your estimates in the boxes. Do not figure out the exact answer, just the estimated answer.

7.
$$
\begin{array}{r}
\underline{27} \\
+\ \underline{32} \\
\hline
\end{array}
$$

8.
$$
\begin{array}{r}
\underline{88} \\
+\ \underline{\ 9} \\
\hline
\end{array}
$$

9.
$$
\begin{array}{r}
\underline{21} \\
+\ \underline{15} \\
\hline
\end{array}
$$

10.
$$
\begin{array}{r}
\underline{75} \\
-\ \underline{11} \\
\hline
\end{array}
$$

11.
$$
\begin{array}{r}
\underline{42} \\
-\ \underline{12} \\
\hline
\end{array}
$$

12.
$$
\begin{array}{r}
\underline{39} \\
-\ \underline{18} \\
\hline
\end{array}
$$

$$
\begin{array}{r}
53 \\
+1\,5 \\
\hline
\end{array}
\qquad
\begin{array}{r}
62 \\
-\ 25 \\
\hline
\end{array}
\qquad
\begin{array}{r}
37 \\
+\ 41 \\
\hline
\end{array}
\qquad
\begin{array}{r}
73 \\
-55 \\
\hline
\end{array}
$$

$$
\begin{array}{r}
123 \\
+249 \\
\hline
\end{array}
\qquad
\begin{array}{r}
615 \\
-399 \\
\hline
\end{array}
\qquad
\begin{array}{r}
573 \\
-262 \\
\hline
\end{array}
$$

The correct estimates for problems 7-12 are written in the boxes below. Check your estimates, and if you answered some incorrectly, review how to estimate to understand why these answers were incorrect.

Now, figure out the exact answer. Then circle the letter beside the exact answer. Use your estimated answer to check your work.

7.

$\begin{array}{r} 27 \\ + 32 \\ \hline \end{array}$ $\begin{array}{r} 30 \\ 30 \\ \hline 60 \end{array}$

a. 39   b. 41   c. 59   d. 69

The correct answer is close to 60. You can cross out 39 and 41.

8.

$\begin{array}{r} 88 \\ + \ 9 \\ \hline \end{array}$ $\begin{array}{r} 90 \\ 10 \\ \hline 100 \end{array}$

a. 74   b. 82   c. 97   d. 120

Use your estimates to cross out wrong answers.

9.

$\begin{array}{r} 21 \\ + 15 \\ \hline \end{array}$ $\begin{array}{r} 20 \\ 20 \\ \hline 40 \end{array}$

a. 36   b. 50   c. 69   d. 76

10.

$\begin{array}{r} 75 \\ - 11 \\ \hline \end{array}$ $\begin{array}{r} 80 \\ 10 \\ \hline 70 \end{array}$

a. 42   b. 53   c. 64   d. 84

The correct answer is close to 70. You can cross out 42 and 84.

11.

$\begin{array}{r} 42 \\ - 12 \\ \hline \end{array}$ $\begin{array}{r} 40 \\ 10 \\ \hline 30 \end{array}$

a. 14   b. 20   c. 22   d. 30

12.

$\begin{array}{r} 39 \\ - 18 \\ \hline \end{array}$ $\begin{array}{r} 40 \\ 20 \\ \hline 20 \end{array}$

a. 12   b. 21   c. 29   d. 30

Congratulations! You know how to estimate answers.
If you would like to practice with more difficult problems, you can go on to the Advanced Guided Practice. However, if you would like to stop here, that is fine.

© 2013 The Critical Thinking Co.™ • www.CriticalThinking.com • 800-458-4849

Advanced Guided Practice

Estimate each number to the nearest 100 or 1,000, and then estimate the total. Write your estimates in the boxes. <u>Do not figure out the exact answer, just the estimated answer</u>.

13.

$$
\begin{array}{r}
\underline{1}21 \\
+ \ \underline{\ }99 \\
\hline
\end{array}
$$

14.

$$
\begin{array}{r}
\underline{2},895 \\
+ \ \underline{3},174 \\
\hline
\end{array}
$$

15.

$$
\begin{array}{r}
\underline{8}13 \\
- \ \underline{5}51 \\
\hline
\end{array}
$$

16.

$$
\begin{array}{r}
\underline{7},928 \\
- \ \underline{4},465 \\
\hline
\end{array}
$$

The correct estimates for problems 13-16 are written in the boxes below. Check your estimates, and if you answered some incorrectly, review how to estimate numbers to understand why these answers were incorrect.

Now, figure out each exact answer. Then circle the letter beside the exact answer. Use your estimated answer to check your work.

13.

$$\begin{array}{r} \underline{1}21 \\ + \ \underline{9}9 \\ \hline \end{array}$$

| 100 |
| 100 |
| 200 |

a. 120   b. 150   c. 180   d. 220

14.

$$\begin{array}{r} \underline{2},895 \\ + \ \underline{3},174 \\ \hline \end{array}$$

| 3,000 |
| 3,000 |
| 6,000 |

a. 5,028   b. 5,642   c. 6,069   d. 6,672

15.

$$\begin{array}{r} \underline{8}13 \\ - \ \underline{5}51 \\ \hline \end{array}$$

| 800 |
| 600 |
| 200 |

a. 202   b. 262   c. 382   d. 422

16.

$$\begin{array}{r} \underline{7},928 \\ - \ \underline{4},465 \\ \hline \end{array}$$

| 8,000 |
| 4,000 |
| 4,000 |

a. 2,742   b. 3,463   c. 4,895   d. 6,032

© 2013 The Critical Thinking Co.™ • www.CriticalThinking.com • 800-458-4849

IX. Solve Complicated Word Problems

When you see a word problem, usually you read it, figure out the math, and then give an answer. That is okay when word problems are simple. **However, what happens when word problems are complicated and confusing?**

In this section you will practice using four steps that can help you solve complicated word problems like the one below.

There are 12 kids on the soccer team and 7 of them are girls. Four kids are goalies. How many boys are on the team?

Step 1: Underline the question that you will need to answer.

As you read the problem, underline the question that you will need to answer. You already know how to underline what's important whenever you read a passage. You're going to be doing that for word problems, too.

Every word problem asks you a question or tells you what to find. When you read a word problem, underline the question that you will need to answer or the part of the problem that tells you what you need to find.

There are 12 kids on the soccer team and 7 of them are girls. Four kids are goalies. How many boys are on the team?

Step 2: List the facts (label each number).

List the facts that you will need in order to find the answer. The facts are numbers and words that describe the numbers.

12 kids on the team   ← Facts are numbers and words that describe the numbers.
 7 girls on the team

Sometimes word problems give you numbers and other information that you do not need in order to find the answer. It is important to know that you may not need to use all the information that is part of the word problem in order to find the answer. You will learn which facts are important to include in your list and which facts are not.

There is a fact in this word problem that you don't need to know. What is it?
I don't need to know that four of the kids are goalies. That does not help me figure out how many boys are on the team!

In Step 3, you will be using your facts to write math sentences.

© 2013 The Critical Thinking Co.™ • www.CriticalThinking.com • 800-458-4849

Step 3: Write a math sentence. Label your answer.

Use your list of facts to <u>write a math sentence</u>. Writing a correct math sentence will lead you to the correct answer.

12 kids on the team – 7 girls on the team = 5 ← boys who are on the team

Labeling your answer is important because you will want to compare it to the question you underlined in Step 1. This way you can be sure you have answered the question you were supposed to answer.

In a math sentence, instead of words, you will use *numbers* and *math operations*.

Math operations are: addition (+), subtraction (-), multiplication (×), and division (÷).

For this word problem, the correct math operation is subtraction.

These charts list key words in word problems that can sometimes tell you which operation to use.

Addition Words	Subtraction Words	Division Words	Multiplication Words
and total in all combined	lost, owe fewer difference of how many left how many more	half (divide by 2) how many groups how many in each	twice as many (x2) of total in all

Practice Choosing the Correct Math Operation

Read each of these simple word problems. Choose the math sentence below that has the correct math operation, and write it in on the line.

1. David had 4 lollipops. Sarah gave him two more. <u>How many lollipops does David have in all</u>?

   _____

2. David had 4 lollipops. He gave two of them to Sarah. <u>How many lollipops did David have left</u>?

   _____

3. David has 4 lollipops. Sarah has twice as many lollipops as David. <u>How many lollipops does Sarah have</u>?

   _____

4. David had 4 lollipops. He gave half of them to Sarah. <u>How many lollipops does David have left</u>?

   _____

a. $4 + 2 = 6$ b. $4 - 2 = 2$ c. $4 \times 2 = 8$ d. $4 \div 2 = 2$

The correct answers for the simple word problems are: 1. a, 2. b, 3. c, 4. d.

© 2013 The Critical Thinking Co.™ • www.CriticalThinking.com • 800-458-4849

Step 4: Check your answer.

Make sure you answered the question that you underlined in Step 1.

There are 12 kids on the soccer team and 7 of them are girls. Four kids are goalies. <u>How many boys are on the team</u>?

12 kids on the team – 7 girls on the team = 5 ← <u>boys on the team</u>

My answer makes sense. The number of boys on the team is exactly what the underlined part of the problem tells me that I should find.

Even students who are very good at math can make mistakes when they don't think about the label that should be on the answer to the word problem. Students need to compare their answer to the question that they were supposed to answer (which they underlined in Step 1). This is especially important when there are two or more math sentences that are needed to solve the problem.

Question: "Okay, when I practice, I have to write the facts in a list. I also have to label the answers. It seems like I'm writing a lot of words. Do I have to write all these words when I take a test?"

Answer: "No! It's important to write words when you practice word problems. However, on a real test, you will *think* about the words, but you will not have to *write* them."

To save time on a test, you don't always have to write words to solve word problems. However, when you practice by writing facts and labeling answers, you are making sure that you know how to think clearly about word problems, which will help you on a test.

Question: "What do I do if I feel confused about a word problem?"

Answer: "If you feel confused when you are working on a word problem, do not think, 'I can't do it.' Instead, make sure you are writing facts and labeling your answer!

12 Kids on the Team   7 Girls   5 Boys

Some students **draw pictures** if they feel confused. This is a good thing to do, especially if the numbers are small. Even when you draw pictures, you should write labels on what you draw."

In the Guided Practice, you are going to practice the four steps.

Guided Practice

Step 1: Underline the question you will need to answer.
Step 2: List the facts (label each number).
Step 3: Write a math sentence. Label your answer.
Step 4: Check your answer.

Now you will be guided through word problems step by step.

It's not just about answering a problem correctly. This is only PART of what needs to be done. The most important thing is to think about how word problems work. You will be asked questions about each word problem that not only lead you to the correct answer but also help you think about how word problems work.

You might not understand some of the word problems right away, but after you see the solution, you can go back and solve the problems again.

"It takes a lot of time to write a fact list and label answers in practice. However, on a test, this practice will help me to understand word problems. On a test, I don't need to write fact lists and label answers like I do when I practice. But when I practice by writing fact lists and labeling answers, it will be easier for me to think through word problems on tests."

© 2013 The Critical Thinking Co.™ • www.CriticalThinking.com • 800-458-4849

Exercise 1

Mr. Green has 3 orange trees and 2 apple trees. He picked 11 apples from each of the two apple trees. How many apples did Mr. Green pick altogether?

Circle the correct answer: 33   30   22   19

Step 1: Underline the question that you will need to answer.

Step 2: List the facts (label each number).
Label the numbers and facts that you will need in order to find the answer.

There is a fact in this word problem that you <u>don't</u> need to know. What is it?

I don't need to know that Mr. Green has 3 orange trees.
I should not use the number 3 in my math sentence.

Step 3: Write a math sentence. Label your answer.

Step 4: Check your answer.

Stuck? Write labels for all the numbers. Still stuck? Please turn the page for the solution.

Solution

Mr. Green has 3 orange trees and 2 apple trees. He picked 11 apples from each of the two apple trees. <u>How many apples did Mr. Green Pick altogether</u>?

Circle the correct answer: 33   30   (22)   19

Step 1: Underline the question that you will need to answer.

Step 2: List the facts (label each number).

    2 apple trees
    11 apples in each tree

> Another way to list the facts is:
>
>   11 apples from the first tree
>   + 11 apples from the second tree

Step 3: Write a math sentence. Label your answer.

2 apple trees × 11 apples in each tree = 22 ← apples that Mr. Green picked altogether

> Another way to solve the problem is:
>
>   11 apples from the first tree
>   + 11 apples from the second tree
>   = 22 ← apples that Mr. Green picked altogether

Step 4: Check your answer.

The number of apples that Mr. Green picked altogether is exactly what the underlined part of the problem tells me I should find.

> **Common Mistakes**
>
> • Some students don't understand that they <u>don't</u> need to know that Mr. Green has 3 orange trees. Then, they write an incorrect math sentence and get the wrong answer.
>
> • Some students may be confused with the words "11 apples from each of the 2 apple trees." These words are another way of saying that Mr. Green has 2 apple trees, and that he picked 11 apples from one tree, and then another 11 apples from the other tree.

If you did not answer the problem correctly, try again.

© 2013 The Critical Thinking Co.™ • www.CriticalThinking.com • 800-458-4849

Exercise 2

Claire went to a farm to visit a horse named Sancho. Claire brought along a bag full of 10 carrots. When she got to the farm, she saw that Sancho was sharing his pasture with a new horse named Scout. She fed both horses the same number of carrots. How many carrots did each horse eat?

Circle the correct answer: 2   3   4   5

Step 1: Underline the question that you will need to answer.

Step 2: List the facts (label each number).

Step 3: Write a math sentence. Label your answer.

Step 4: Check your answer.

Stuck? Write labels for all the numbers. Still stuck? Please turn the page for the solution.

Solution

Claire went to a farm to visit a horse named Sancho. Claire brought along a bag full of 10 carrots. When she got to the farm, she saw that Sancho was sharing his pasture with a new horse named Scout. She fed both horses the same number of carrots. <u>How many carrots did each horse eat</u>?

Circle the correct answer: 2   3   4   ⑤

Step 1: Underline the question that you will need to answer.

Step 2: List the facts (label each number).

2 horses
10 carrots in the bag

Step 3: Write a math sentence. Label your answer.

I need to know that both horses got the same number of carrots. Another way to say that is that the 10 carrots were divided equally between the 2 horses.

10 ÷ 2 = 5 ←each horse ate 5 carrots

If there are 10 carrots and 2 horses, that means that each horse ate 5 carrots.

Step 4: Check your answer.

Look at the part of the word problem you underlined. Does your answer and label make sense?

My answer and my answer label make sense.

Common Mistake

Some students don't understand that this is a division problem. Then, they write an incorrect math sentence and the answer is wrong.

If you did not answer the problem correctly, try again.

© 2013 The Critical Thinking Co.™ • www.CriticalThinking.com • 800-458-4849

Exercise 3

Maxwell and his dad baked 2 sheets of 12 cookies. After they took the cookies out of the oven, they left them out to cool and then took a walk. When they returned, they noticed that 6 of the cookies were missing. How many cookies were left?

Circle the correct answer: 18   24   30   36

Step 1: Underline the question that you will need to answer.

Step 2: List the facts (label each number).

Step 3: Write a math sentence. Label your answer.

Step 4: Check your answer.

Stuck? Write labels for all the numbers.   Still stuck? Please turn the page for the solution.

Solution

Maxwell and his dad baked 2 sheets of 12 cookies. After they took the cookies out of the oven, they left them out to cool and then took a walk. When they returned, they noticed that 6 of the cookies were missing. <u>How many cookies were left</u>?

Circle the correct answer: 18   24   30   36

Step 1: Underline the question that you will need to answer.

Step 2: List the facts (label each number).

2 sheets
12 cookies on each sheet
6 cookies were missing

Step 3: Write a math sentence. Label your answer.

2 × 12 = 24 cookies total
24 cookies total – 6 cookies missing = 18 cookies left

Here's a picture of the problem:

12 + 12 cookies baked - 6 missing = <u>18 cookies left</u>

Step 4: Check your answer.

The part of the word problem that I underlined asks, "How many cookies were left?" The answer is that 18 cookies were left. I know that the answer cannot be 30 or 36, because they baked only 24 cookies, so I can cross out 30 and 36.

Common Mistakes

- Some students think the correct answer is 24. They figure out that there were 24 cookies total, but then they forget to subtract the 6 cookies that were missing. They write one math sentence: 2 × 12 = 24 cookies total, but then they forget to write the second math sentence: 24 cookies total - 6 cookies missing = 18 cookies left.

- Some students get confused with the words and are helped by drawing a picture to see the word problem. Remember, even pictures need to have labels.

If you did not answer the problem correctly, try again.

    © 2013 The Critical Thinking Co.™ • www.CriticalThinking.com • 800-458-4849

Exercise 4

Stan, Kyle, and Eric are three brothers. Their father gave them a 2 pound bag of 30 pretzels and said, "I want you boys to share the bag evenly among you so that you each have the same number." How many pretzels did each boy get?

Circle the correct answer: 3   10   30   90

Step 1: Underline the question that you will need to answer.

Step 2: List the facts (label each number).

There is a fact in this word problem that you <u>don't</u> need to know. What is it?

_____

_____

Step 3: Write a math sentence. Label your answer.

Step 4: Check your answer.

Stuck? Write labels for all the numbers. Still stuck? Please turn the page for the solution.

© 2013 The Critical Thinking Co.™ • www.CriticalThinking.com • 800-458-4849

Solution

Stan, Kyle, and Eric are three brothers. Their father gave them a 2 pound bag of 30 pretzels and said, "I want you boys to share the bag evenly among you so that you each have the same number." <u>How many pretzels did each boy get</u>?

Circle the correct answer: 3   (10)   30   90

Step 1: Underline the question that you will need to answer.

Step 2: List the facts (label each number).

30 pretzels
3 boys

> There is a fact in this word problem that you <u>don't</u> need to know. What is it?

I don't need to know that the bag weighs 2 pounds. The number 2 is not part of the problem.

Step 3: Write a math sentence. Label your answer.

30 pretzels ÷ 3 boys = 10 ← each boy gets 10 pretzels

Here's a picture of the problem:

<u>The bag has 30 pretzels.</u>   ↙ ↓ ↘   <u>Each boy gets the same number of pretzels.</u>

<u>Each boy gets 10 pretzels.</u>

Step 4: Check your answer.

Each boy got 10 pretzels. That makes sense.

Common Mistakes

- The number "3" is written out as a word, so some students forget to list and label the "3 boys" who will be sharing the pretzels.

- Some students don't understand that this is a division problem. The words "share the bag evenly among you" tells you that the bag will be divided among the 3 boys.

- Another way to tell that it is a division problem is to draw a picture with labels on what's in the picture. The picture shows you that the word problem is asking you to divide the bag among the three boys.

> If you did not answer the problem correctly, try again.

© 2013 The Critical Thinking Co.™ • www.CriticalThinking.com • 800-458-4849

Exercise 5

Lucky is a dog who begs for snacks. Andy gave Lucky 2 snacks. Shira gave Lucky 3 snacks. Then, Lucky found 3 more snacks that someone spilled. Before he could eat all 3 snacks, Shira took 2 away saying, "If you eat too many snacks, you'll get a belly ache!" How many snacks did Lucky eat?

Circle the correct answer: 4   5   6   7

Step 1: Underline the question that you will need to answer.

Step 2: List the facts (label each number).

Step 3: Write a math sentence. Label your answer.

Step 4: Check your answer.

Stuck? Write labels for all the numbers. Still stuck? Please turn the page for the solution.

Solution

Lucky is a dog who begs for snacks. Andy gave Lucky 2 snacks. Shira gave Lucky 3 snacks. Then, Lucky found 3 more snacks that someone spilled. Before he could eat all 3 snacks, Shira took 2 away saying, "If you eat too many snacks, you'll get a belly ache!" <u>How many snacks did Lucky eat</u>?

Circle the correct answer: 4   5   ⑥   7

Step 1: Underline the question that you will need to answer.

Step 2: List the facts (label each number).

2 snacks that Andy gave Lucky
3 snacks that Shira gave Lucky
3 snacks that spilled
2 snacks that spilled that Lucky did not eat (I will need to subtract 2 snacks)

Step 3: Write a math sentence. Label your answer.

2 (snacks from Andy) + 3 (snacks from Shira) = 5 snacks Lucky ate

But Lucky had more than 5 snacks. He started to eat 3 snacks that someone had spilled, but before he could eat all 3, Shira took away 2.

3 (snacks that spilled that Lucky tried to eat) – 2 (snacks Shira took away) = 1 snack Lucky ate

So, Lucky ate 5 snacks that Andy and Shira gave him, and then he ate 1 more from the snacks that someone had spilled.

5 + 1 = 6 ←total number of snacks that Lucky ate

Step 4: Check your answer.

My answer label and the other labels I used all make sense. I found the number of snacks that Lucky ate.

Common Mistake

It's easy to get confused with this problem because the list of numbers is long, and the numbers all have different labels. Most of the labels tell you to add, but there is one that tells you to subtract (the number of snacks that spilled that Lucky did <u>not</u> eat). When students make a mistake on this problem, it helps them to think through the facts and the labels for each number.

If you did not answer the problem correctly, try again.

© 2013 The Critical Thinking Co.™ • www.CriticalThinking.com • 800-458-4849

For this exercise there are no reminders about how to use the steps. Use the steps without reminders. If you forgot the steps, turn the page and look at the solution for help.

Exercise 6

Kamal's grandma measured his height a few years ago. There is a mark on a wall in their home that reads, "Kamal, 46 inches." Yesterday, Kamal's grandma measured him again and said, "Wow! You are now 53 inches tall!" How many inches has Kamal grown?

Circle the correct answer: 3 inches   53 inches   7 inches $4\frac{1}{2}$ inches

Stuck? Write labels for all the numbers. Still stuck? Please turn the page for the solution.

Solution

Kamal's grandma measured his height a few years ago. There is a mark on a wall in their home that reads, "Kamal, 46 inches." Yesterday, Kamal's grandma measured him again and said, "Wow! You are now 53 inches tall!" <u>How many inches has Kamal grown</u>?

Circle the correct answer: 3 inches   53 inches   (7 inches)   4 $\frac{1}{2}$ inches

Step 1: Underline the question that you will need to answer.

Step 2: List the facts (label each number).

> 46 inches a few years ago
> 53 inches now

Step 3: Write a math sentence. Label your answer.

> 53 – 46 = 7← inches Kamal has grown

Step 4: Check your answer.

> The part of the word problem that I underlined asks, "How many inches has Kamal grown?" The answer is that Kamal has grown 7 inches.

If you did not answer the problem correctly, try again.

© 2013 The Critical Thinking Co.™ • www.CriticalThinking.com • 800-458-4849

Use the steps without reminders. Remember to **use estimation** to solve the problem and to check you work.

Exercise 7

Samira had a $10.00 bill to spend in a toy store. She bought one unicorn figurine for $4.99 and one book of stickers for $1.89. How much change did she get back from her $10.00?

Circle the correct answer: $6.88 $3.12 $3.98 $5.01

Stuck? Write labels for all the numbers. Still stuck? Please turn the page for the solution.

Solution

Samira had a $10.00 bill to spend in a toy store. She bought one unicorn figurine for $4.99 and one book of stickers for $1.89. <u>How much change did she get back from her $10.00?</u>

Circle the correct answer: $6.88   ($3.12) $3.98 $5.01

Step 1: Underline the question that you will need to answer.

Step 2: List the facts (label each number).

$10.00 Samira had to spend
$4.99 cost of unicorn
$1.89 cost of stickers

Step 3: Write a math sentence. Label your answer.

$4.99   cost of unicorn
+ $1.89   cost of stickers
$6.88 ← cost of the unicorn and the stickers.

Now I need to subtract $6.88 from $10.00 to find out how much change she will get back.

$10.00
- $6.88
$3.12 ← change that she will get back from $10.00.

Step 4: Check your answer.

My answer label and the other labels I wrote make sense, and I answered the question that was underlined.

Now, I want to check my work by using estimation.

$4.99 is about $5.00. $1.89 is about $2.00.

Her toys are about $7.00. If she pays for them with a $10.00 bill, then she should get about $3.00 back in change. That's very close to $3.12.

Common Mistakes

- Some students figure out the total price of the unicorn and the stickers, which is $6.88. Then, they give $6.88 as their answer. They do not carefully read the underlined sentence. The underlined sentence tells you to <u>subtract</u> $6.88 from $10.00 in order to figure out how much change she got back.

- When working with big numbers with lots of digits, it's easy to make a mistake. Using estimation can help you catch mistakes when you work with big numbers.

If you did not answer the problem correctly, try again.

Congratulations! You have learned how to do your best while working difficult word problems. If you didn't get a problem right the first time and then tried it a second time, you should be very proud of yourself for trying again. Good students don't always get all the questions right, but they stick with it and try again.

If you would like to practice with more difficult word problems, you can go on to Advanced Guided Practice. However, if you would like to stop here, that is fine.

© 2013 The Critical Thinking Co.™ • www.CriticalThinking.com • 800-458-4849

Advanced Guided Practice

Exercise 8

Three dragons, Albert, Bertha, and Drake, were having a contest to see who could breathe fire the farthest. Albert breathed a line of fire that was 25 feet long. Bertha breathed a line of fire that was three times as long as Albert's. But Drake won the contest, breathing a line of fire that was 100 feet long. How long was Bertha's line of fire?

Circle the correct answer: 50 feet   75 feet   100 feet   125 feet

Step 1: Underline the question that you will need to answer.

Step 2: List the facts (label each number).

> There is a fact in this word problem that you <u>don't</u> need to know. What is it?

_____

_____

Step 3: Write a math sentence. Label your answer.

Step 4: Check your answer.

> Stuck? Write labels for all the numbers. Still stuck? Please turn the page for the solution.

Solution

Three dragons, Albert, Bertha, and Drake, were having a contest to see who could breathe fire the farthest. Albert breathed a line of fire that was 25 feet long. Bertha breathed a line of fire that was three times as long as Albert's. But Drake won the contest, breathing a line of fire that was 100 feet long. <u>How long was Bertha's line of fire</u>?

Circle the correct answer: 50 feet   75 feet   100 feet   125 feet

Step 1: Underline the question that you will need to answer.

Step 2: List the facts (label each number).

25 feet ←Albert's line of fire
Bertha's line was 3 times as long as Albert's.

There is a fact in this word problem that you <u>don't</u> need to know. What is it?

To write the math sentence, I don't need to know that Drake breathed a line of fire that was 100 feet long or that he won the contest. But I can use the information about Drake to cross out wrong answers. Because Drake won the contest, Bertha's line of fire has to be less than 100 feet long. So I can cross out the last 2 answer choices.

Step 3: Write a math sentence. Label your answer.

25 feet × 3 = 75 feet ←length of Bertha's line of fire

Step 4: Check your answer.

My answer label makes sense. The answer is 75 feet, which is one of the answer choices.

Common Mistake

Some students don't understand that they <u>don't</u> need to know anything about Drake in order to write the math sentence. If they use the wrong information in the math sentence, then their answer is wrong.

If you did not answer the problem correctly, try again.

Exercise 9

Billy used to have 10 game cards. Last week, he bought new game cards. Billy's friend, Amir, went to the same store and bought 6 new game cards. Amir now has 17 game cards. Billy now has 5 fewer game cards than Amir. How many new game cards did Billy buy last week?

Circle the correct answer: 2   7   12   13

Step 1: Underline the question that you will need to answer.

Step 2: List the facts (label each number).

> There is a fact in this word problem that you <u>don't</u> need to know. What is it?

_____

_____

Step 3: Write a math sentence. Label your answer.

Step 4: Check your answer.

> Stuck? Write labels for all the numbers. Still stuck? Please turn the page for the solution.

Solution

Billy used to have 10 game cards. Last week, he bought new game cards. Billy's friend, Amir, went to the same store and bought 6 new game cards. Amir now has 17 game cards. Billy now has 5 fewer game cards than Amir. <u>How many new game cards did Billy buy last week</u>?

Circle the correct answer: (2)   7   12   13

Step 1: Underline the question that you will need to answer.

Step 2: List the facts (label each number).

10 game cards Billy used to have
17 game cards Amir has
5 fewer then Amir ← the number of game cards that Billy has now

There is a fact in this word problem that you <u>don't</u> need to know. What is it?

I don't need to know that Amir bought 6 game cards.

Step 3: Write a math sentence. Label your answer.

17 – 5 = 12 ← game cards Billy has now

Look at the underlined part of the word problem. I need to find out how many new game cards Billy bought last week.
If he has 12 game cards now, and he used to have 10 game cards, then:
12 – 10 = 2 ← new game cards Billy bought last week.

Step 4: Check your answer.

I looked at the underlined part of the word problem and figured out how many new game cards Billy bought last week. My answer label makes sense.

Common Mistake

Some students write only one math sentence: 17 – 5 = 12 ← game cards Billy has now. Then, they think that 12 is the correct answer. However, if you read the underlined part of the problem, you know that you are supposed to find the number of <u>new</u> game cards that Billy bought last week. That means you have to subtract the number of game cards that Billy had last week from the number of game cards that Billy has now: 12 – 10 = 2 ← new game cards Billy bought last week. That's the answer label that makes sense.

If you did not answer the problem correctly, try again.

© 2013 The Critical Thinking Co.™ • www.CriticalThinking.com • 800-458-4849

For the rest of the exercises there are no reminders, except in the solutions.

Exercise 10

Mr. Kramden drives a bus. At his first stop, 21 people got on his empty bus. At his second stop, 8 people got off, and 4 people got on. How many people were riding Mr. Kramden's bus after the second stop?

Circle the correct answer: 8   13   17   21

Stuck? Write labels for all the numbers. Still stuck? Please turn the page for the solution.

Solution

Mr. Kramden drives a bus. At his first stop, 21 people got on his empty bus. At his second stop, 8 people got off, and 4 people got on. <u>How many people were riding Mr. Kramden's bus after the second stop</u>?

Circle the correct answer: 8   13   (17)   21

Step 1: Underline the question that you will need to answer.

Step 2: List the facts (label each number).

21 people got on at the first stop.
8 people got off at the second stop.
4 people got on at the second stop.

Step 3: Write a math sentence. Label your answer.

At the second stop, there were 21 people on the bus, but 8 people got off.
21 – 8 = 13 ← people on the bus

Then, 4 new people got on.
13 + 4 = 17 ← people riding the bus after the second stop

Another way to solve the problem is:
At the second stop, 8 people got off, but then 4 new people got on. So that means that the total number of people who got off at the second stop is:
8 – 4 = 4 ← total number of people who got off at the second stop

There were 21 people on the bus before the second stop, but then a total of 4 people got off:
21 – 4 = 17 ← <u>people riding the bus after the second stop</u>

Step 4: Check your answer.

My label makes sense. I found out how many people were on the bus after the second stop.

Common Mistake

It's easy to get confused with this problem because the list of numbers is long, and the numbers all have different labels. Most of the labels tell you to add, but there are some that tell you to subtract. When kids make a mistake on this problem, it helps them to think through the list of numbers and the labels for each number.

If you did not answer the problem correctly, try again.

 © 2013 The Critical Thinking Co.™ • www.CriticalThinking.com • 800-458-4849

Exercise 11 ————————————————————————————

Adult Dalmatian dogs usually have about 90 spots. Dalmatian puppies that are only 1 month old usually have about 60 spots. How many more spots would a group of 4 adult dogs have when compared to a group of 4 puppies?

Circle the correct answer: 360   240   120   60

Stuck? Write labels for all the numbers. Still stuck? Please turn the page for the solution.

Solution

Adult Dalmatian dogs usually have about 90 spots. Dalmatian puppies that are only 1 month old usually have about 60 spots. <u>How many more spots would a group of 4 adult dogs have when compared to a group of 4 puppies</u>?

Circle the correct answer: 360   240   (120)   60

Step 1: Underline the question that you will need to answer.

Step 2: List the facts (label each number).

4 adult dogs that have 90 spots each

4 puppies that have 60 spots each

I need to know how many more spots are in the group of adult dogs when compared to the group of puppies.

Step 3: Write a math sentence. Label your answer.

4 × 90 = 360 ← number of spots in the group of adult dogs

4 × 60 = 240 ← number of spots in the group of puppies

360 – 240 = 120 ← the group of adult dogs has 120 more spots than the group of puppies

Step 4: Check your answer.

My answer labels make sense, and I answered the question that was underlined.

Common Mistake

It's important that you understand you are subtracting the total number of spots in the puppy group from the total number of spots in the adult dog group. Once you figure out the number of spots in each group, it is a subtraction problem.

If you did not answer the problem correctly, try again.

Exercise 12

A cheetah can run a mile in only 70 seconds. That is very fast! A white-tailed deer is also fast but not as fast as a cheetah. A cheetah needs only half the time that a white-tailed deer needs to run a mile. How many seconds does a white-tailed deer need to run a mile?

Circle the correct answer: 35 seconds   120 seconds   140 seconds   210 seconds

Stuck? Write labels for all the numbers. Still stuck? Please turn the page for the solution.

Solution

A cheetah can run a mile in only 70 seconds. That is very fast! A white-tailed deer is also fast but not as fast as a cheetah. A cheetah needs only half the time that a white-tailed deer needs to run a mile. <u>How many seconds does a white-tailed deer need to run a mile</u>?

Circle the correct answer: 35 seconds   120 seconds   (140 seconds)   210 seconds

Step 1: Underline the question that you will need to answer.

Step 2: List the facts (label each number).

70 seconds is the time it takes a cheetah to run a mile.

A cheetah needs only half the time that a white-tailed deer needs to run a mile.

Step 3: Write a math sentence. Label your answer.

The word problem has the word "half." When something is "half," that means it is divided by 2.

If a cheetah needs half the time of a white-tailed deer, then that means that a white-tailed deer takes twice as long as a cheetah.

I don't need to divide by 2, I need to multiply by 2.

70 seconds (the time a cheetah needs) × 2 = 140 ←seconds a white-tailed deer needs

> Another way to solve the problem is to use algebra:
> seconds a white-tailed deer needs ÷ 2 = 70 seconds (the time a cheetah needs)
> seconds a white-tailed deer needs = 70 seconds (the time a cheetah needs) × 2
> seconds a white-tailed deer needs = 140 seconds

Step 4: Check your answer.

My answer makes sense. I found the number of seconds the white-tailed deer needs to run a mile. I know that 35 seconds cannot be correct. If a white-tailed deer needed only 35 seconds, then it would be faster than a cheetah, which is not correct.

> **Common Mistake**
>
> This problem is tricky because it uses the word "half," which is a division word. Some students write the number sentence 70 ÷ 2 = 35 and believe that 35 seconds is the amount of time that a white-tailed deer needs to run a mile. However, if you think about that answer, it must be wrong, because that would mean a white-tailed deer is faster than a cheetah.

If you did not answer the problem correctly, try again.

© 2013 The Critical Thinking Co.™ • www.CriticalThinking.com • 800-458-4849

X. Different Units of Measure in Word Problems

If you compare the value of **1 nickel** to that of **3 pennies**, 1 is more than 3.

If you compare the length of **1 foot** to that of **3 inches**, 1 is more than 3.

One is more than 3 if you compare <u>different units of measure</u>. Comparing different units of measure in a word problem is complicated, like a riddle. To make things easier when taking a test, you should not compare different units of measure. You should compare the <u>same units of measure</u>.

If you compare the **same** units of measure, then it's easy to see that:

5 cents is more than 3 cents.

And 12 inches is more than 3 inches.

To work with **different** units of measure: Change your facts so that all the numbers have the <u>same</u> unit of measure.

Look at this word problem:

Eddie has 1 nickel and 3 pennies in his pocket. How much money does he have?

Let's use the steps you've already practiced to solve the word problem.

Step 1: Underline the question that you will need to answer.

First, you underline "How much money does he have?"

Step 2: List the facts (label each number).

Then list the facts (label each number) like this:

1 nickel
3 pennies

Step 3: Write a math sentence. Label your answer.

Now, when you write a math sentence, do you add 1 + 3 to see how much money Eddie has? **No, you do not!**

Adding 1 + 3 would lead you to the wrong answer.

To get the right answer, you have to **change the numbers** so that they are all the **same unit of measure** before you add them.

© 2013 The Critical Thinking Co.™ • www.CriticalThinking.com • 800-458-4849

Let's look at the word problem again and solve it the right way:

Eddie has 1 nickel and 3 pennies in his pocket. How much money does Eddie have?

Step 1: Underline the question that you will need to answer.

First, you underline "How much money does Eddie have?"

Step 2: List the facts (label each number).

Then list the facts (label each number) like this:

1 nickel
3 pennies

Before you use these facts in a math sentence, you have to change the numbers so that all the numbers in the list have the **same unit of measure**. The unit of measure is **cents**.

Facts	Facts With Same Unit of Measure
1 nickel 3 pennies	5 cents 3 cents

Step 3: Write a math sentence. Label your answer.

Now that you have the correct facts, you can write a math sentence.

5 + 3 = 8 cents ← This is how much money Eddie has.

Step 4: Check your answer.

Does the answer label make sense?

Yes, it does!

It's important to use the same unit of measure for every number before you write your math sentence. Otherwise, you might think that Eddie has only 4 cents in his pocket!

In this exercise, you will practice changing numbers so that all the numbers in the list have the same unit of measure.

Usually you will change the numbers to the <u>smallest unit of measure</u>. For example, if you have "1 minute" and "17 seconds," you will change the minute into seconds because seconds is the <u>smallest unit of measure</u>.

Complete the table. The first three have been done for you.

Facts	Facts With Same Unit of Measure
1 minute 17 seconds	60 seconds 17 seconds
1 dozen eggs 3 eggs	12 eggs 3 eggs
1 pound (hint: 1 pound = 16 ounces) 7 ounces	16 ounces 7 ounces
1 kilogram (hint: 1 kilogram = 1,000 grams) 252 grams	
1 meter (hint: 1 meter = 100 centimeters) 76 centimeters	
1 yard (hint: 1 yard = 3 feet) 2 feet	
1 week (hint: 1 week = 7 days) 4 days	

For answers, see page 138.

© 2013 The Critical Thinking Co.™ • www.CriticalThinking.com • 800-458-4849

Sometimes, you will have to do multiplication when you change numbers. In this exercise, you will practice multiplying in order to change numbers so that all the numbers in the list have the same unit of measure.

Complete the table. The first three have been done for you.

Facts	(Multiplication)	Facts With Same Unit of Measure
3 quarters 1 dime	3 x 25 = 75	75 cents 10 cents
3 feet (hint: 1 foot = 12 inches) 5 inches	3 x 12 = 36	36 inches 5 inches
2 pounds (hint: 1 pound = 16 ounces) 7 ounces	2 x 16 = 32	32 ounces 7 ounces
3 weeks (hint: 1 week = 7 days) 5 days		
2 hours (hint: 1 hour = 60 minutes) 43 minutes		
2 dozen eggs (hint: 1 dozen = 12) 5 eggs		
5 gallons (hint: 1 gallon = 4 quarts) 7 quarts		

For answers, please turn the page.

© 2013 The Critical Thinking Co.™ • www.CriticalThinking.com • 800-458-4849

Here are the completed tables. Check your work. If you have an incorrect number, try again.

Facts	Facts With Same Unit of Measure
1 kilogram (hint: 1 kilogram = 1,000 grams) 252 grams	1,000 grams 252 grams
1 meter (hint: 1 meter = 100 centimeters) 76 centimeters	100 centimeters 76 centimeters
1 yard (hint: 1 yard = 3 feet) 2 feet	3 feet 2 feet
1 week (hint: 1 week = 7 days) 4 days	7 days 4 days

Facts	(Multiplication)	Facts With Same Unit of Measure
3 weeks (hint: 1 week = 7 days) 5 days	3 × 7 = 21	21 days 5 days
2 hours (hint: 1 hour = 60 minutes) 43 minutes	2 × 60 = 120	120 minutes 43 minutes
2 dozen eggs (hint: 1 dozen = 12) 5 eggs	2 × 12 = 24	24 eggs 5 eggs
5 gallons (hint: 1 gallon = 4 quarts) 7 quarts	5 × 4 = 20	20 quarts 7 quarts

© 2013 The Critical Thinking Co.™ • www.CriticalThinking.com • 800-458-4849

Guided Practice

When you see units of measure in word problems, you will use the same word problem steps that you've already learned.

> **Step 1:** Underline the question that you will need to answer.
> **Step 2:** List the facts (label each number).
> **Step 3:** Write a math sentence. Label your answer.
> **Step 4:** Check your answer.

However, you will have to <u>change your facts so that all the numbers in the list have the same unit of measure</u>, just as you've already practiced.

These next practice problems will use the steps above to find the solution. After you solve each word problem, you can turn the page to see the solution.

Exercise 1

Mr. Hodgepodge looked underneath the cushions of his couch and found 2 quarters and 4 dimes. How much money did he find?

Circle the correct answer: 50¢   75¢   90¢ $2.40

Step 1: Underline the question that you will need to answer.

Step 2: List the facts (label each number).

Facts	(Multiplication)	Facts With Same Unit of Measure
_____	_____	_____
_____	_____	_____

Step 3: Write a math sentence. Label your answer.

Step 4: Check your answer.

> Stuck? Write labels for all the numbers. Still stuck? Please turn the page for the solution.

© 2013 The Critical Thinking Co.™ • www.CriticalThinking.com • 800-458-4849

Solution

Mr. Hodgepodge looked underneath the cushions of his couch and found 2 quarters and 4 dimes. <u>How much money did he find?</u>

Circle the correct answer: 50¢   75¢   (90¢) $2.40

Step 1: Underline the question that you will need to answer.

Step 2: List the facts (label each number).

Facts	(Multiplication)	Facts With Same Unit of Measure
2 quarters 4 dimes	2 x 25 cents = 50 4 x 10 cents = 40	50 cents in quarters 40 cents in dimes

Step 3: Write a math sentence. Label your answer.

> 50 cents in quarters
> + 40 cents in dimes
> 90 cents ← total amount of money he found

Step 4: Check your answer.

I answered the question I underlined, and the answer is in cents.

Common Mistake

Students sometimes don't understand that in order to change the coins into dollars and cents, they need to use multiplication.

If you did not answer the problem correctly, try again.

© 2013 The Critical Thinking Co.™ • www.CriticalThinking.com • 800-458-4849

Exercise 2

Leo is a huge, 10 pound guinea pig who loves to eat. Leo started the day with 1 kilogram of food in his bowl. By lunchtime, he had eaten 700 grams of his food. How much food was left in his bowl?
(hint: 1 kilogram = 1,000 grams)

Circle the correct answer: 3,000 kilograms   3,000 grams   300 kilograms   300 grams

Step 1: Underline the question that you will need to answer.

Step 2: List the facts (label each number).

Facts	Facts With Same Unit of Measure
_____	_____
_____	_____

There is a fact in this word problem that you __don't__ need to know in order to find the answer. What is it?

_____

_____

Step 3: Write a math sentence. Label your answer.

Step 4: Check your answer.

Stuck? Write labels for all the numbers. Still stuck? Please turn the page for the solution.

© 2013 The Critical Thinking Co.™ • www.CriticalThinking.com • 800-458-4849

olution

Leo is a huge, 10 pound guinea pig who loves to eat. Leo started the day with 1 kilogram of food in his bowl. By lunchtime, he had eaten 700 grams of his food. <u>How much food was left in his bowl</u>? (hint: 1 kilogram = 1,000 grams)

Circle the correct answer: 3,000 kilograms   3,000 grams   300 kilograms   (300 grams)

Step 1: Underline the question that you will need to answer.

Step 2: List the facts (label each number).

Facts	Facts With Same Unit of Measure
1 kilogram 700 grams	1,000 grams at the start of the day 700 grams eaten by lunchtime

There is a fact in this word problem that you <u>don't</u> need to know in order to find the answer. What is it?

I don't need to know that Leo weighs 10 pounds. 10 pounds is not something I can use in a math sentence.

Step 3: Write a math sentence. Label your answer.

1,000 - 700 = 300 ←<u>grams left in his bowl</u>

Step 4: Check your answer.

I answered the question I underlined, and the answer label has the correct unit of measure.

Common Mistake

Students can get confused when they change 1 kilogram to 1,000 grams.

If you did not answer the problem correctly, try again.

         © 2013 The Critical Thinking Co.™ • www.CriticalThinking.com • 800-458-4849

Exercise 3

Brian is going on a trip to visit his aunt for 3 weeks. Then, he will go to visit his uncle for 2 weeks. Finally, he will visit his grandparents for 5 days. How many days in all will Brian visit his aunt, uncle, and grandparents?

Circle the correct answer: 1 month   19 days   21 days   40 days

Step 1: Underline the question that you will need to answer.

Step 2: List the facts (label each number).

Facts	(Multiplication)	Facts With Same Unit of Measure
_____	_____	_____
_____	_____	_____
_____	_____	_____

Step 3: Write a math sentence. Label your answer.

Step 4: Check your answer.

Stuck? Write labels for all the numbers. Still stuck? Please turn the page for the solution.

Solution

Brian is going on a trip to visit his aunt for 3 weeks. Then, he will go to visit his uncle for 2 weeks. Finally, he will visit his grandparents for 5 days. <u>How many days in all will Brian visit his aunt, uncle, and grandparents</u>?

Circle the correct answer: 1 month   19 days   21 days   (40 days)

Step 1: Underline the question that you will need to answer.

Step 2: List the facts (label each number).

Facts	(Multiplication)	Facts With Same Unit of Measure
3 weeks 2 weeks 5 days	3 × 7 = 21 2 × 7 = 14	21 days visiting his aunt 14 days visiting his uncle 5 days visiting his grandparents

Step 3: Write a math sentence. Label your answer.

$$\begin{array}{r} 21 \\ 14 \\ +\ 5 \\ \hline 40 \end{array}$$ ← total number of days visiting his aunt, uncle, and grandparents

Step 4: Check your answer.

I answered the question I underlined, and the answer is in days, which is the correct unit of measure.

If you did not answer the problem correctly, try again.

   © 2013 The Critical Thinking Co.™ • www.CriticalThinking.com • 800-458-4849

Exercise 4

On a farm, the height of a bull's fence is 2 yards and 6 inches. The height of a cow's fence is 6 feet. Which animal has the taller fence? Explain your answer. (hint: 1 yard = 3 feet)

_____

_____

_____

Step 1: Underline the question that you will need to answer.

Step 2: List the facts (label each number).

Facts	(Multiplication)	Facts With Same Unit of Measure
_____	_____	_____
_____	_____	_____

Step 3: Write a math sentence. Label your answer.

You do not need to write a math sentence. Just compare the height of the fences.

Step 4: Check your answer.

Stuck? Write labels for all the numbers. Still stuck? Please turn the page for the solution.

Solution

On a farm, the height of a bull's fence is 2 yards and 6 inches. The height of a cow's fence is 6 feet. <u>Which animal has the taller fence</u>? Explain your answer.
(1 yard = 3 feet)

The bull has the taller fence. If I change 2 yards to 6 feet, then I know that the bull's fence is 6 feet and 6 inches. The cow's fence is only 6 feet.

Step 1: Underline the question that you will need to answer.

Step 2: List the facts (label each number).

Facts	(Multiplication)	Facts With Same Unit of Measure
2 yards and 6 inches 6 feet	2 x 3 = 6 feet	6 feet and 6 inches ← <u>height of bull's fence</u> 6 feet ← <u>height of cow's fence</u>

Step 3: Write a math sentence. Label your answer.

You do not need to write a math sentence. Just compare the height of the fences.

I don't need to do any math, because I just want to compare the height of the bull's fence to the height of the cow's fence.

Now that I have changed the numbers so that they are all the same unit of measure, I can see that the bull has the taller fence.

Step 4: Check your answer.

I answered the question I underlined.

Another way to solve this problem is to change feet into yards:

6 feet ÷ 3 feet = 2 yards. The cow's fence is 2 yards. The bull's fence is taller.

Here's another way to explain the answer:

If I change 6 feet to 2 yards, then I know that the bull's fence is 2 yards and 6 inches, but the cow's fence is only 2 yards.

Common Mistake

The key to this problem is to have the height of the bull's fence and the height of the cow's fence in the same unit of measure. Then, it is easy to compare and to find out that the bull has the taller fence. You do not have to write a math sentence.

If you did not answer the problem correctly, try again.

© 2013 The Critical Thinking Co.™ • www.CriticalThinking.com • 800-458-4849

The steps will not be included in the next exercises, except in the solutions.

Exercise 5

Ms. Bear opened a box of 2 dozen donuts. She and her friends ate all of them!

Ms. Bear went back to the donut shop to buy more, but they had only 7 donuts left. She bought them all. Ms. Bear and her friends ate all 7 of those donuts, too!

What is the total number of donuts that Ms. Bear and her friends ate?

Circle the correct answer: 17   31   40   3 dozen

Stuck? Write labels for all the numbers. Still stuck? Please turn the page for the solution.

© 2013 The Critical Thinking Co.™ • www.CriticalThinking.com • 800-458-4849

Solution

Ms. Bear opened a box of 2 dozen donuts. She and her friends ate all of them!

Ms. Bear went back to the donut shop to buy more, but they had only 7 donuts left. She bought them all. Ms. Bear and her friends ate all 7 of those donuts, too!

<u>What is the total number of donuts that Ms. Bear and her friends ate</u>?

Circle the correct answer: 17   (31)   40   3 dozen

Step 1: Underline the question that you will need to answer.

Step 2: List the facts (label each number).

Facts	(Multiplication)	Facts With Same Unit of Measure
2 dozen donuts 7 donuts	2 × 12 = 24	24 donuts 7 donuts

Step 3: Write a math sentence. Label your answer.

24 + 7 = 31 donuts total

Step 4: Check your answer.

I answered the question I underlined.

If you did not answer the problem correctly, try again.

Congratulations! You have learned how to understand units of measure in word problems. If you didn't get a problem right the first time and then tried it a second time, you should be very proud of yourself for trying again. Remember, good students don't always answer all the questions correctly, but they stick with it and try again.

If you would like to practice with more difficult word problems, you can go on to Advanced Guided Practice. However, if you would like to stop here, that is fine.

© 2013 The Critical Thinking Co.™ • www.CriticalThinking.com • 800-458-4849

Advanced Guided Practice

Exercise 6

A store manager wants to know how long it takes for customers to check out. The manager timed 100 customers in order to figure out the average amount of time it took a customer to check out.

The manager found that the average customer waits in line for 1 minute, then waits at the cash register for 30 seconds while the cashier adds the cost of the items, and finally pays at the cash register for 30 more seconds. How many minutes does it take the average customer to check out?

Circle the correct answer: 150 seconds   120 seconds   2 minutes   3 minutes

Stuck? Write labels for all the numbers. Still stuck? Please turn the page for the solution.

Solution

A store manager wants to know how long it takes for customers to check out. The manager timed 100 customers in order to figure out the average amount of time it took a customer to check out.

The manager found that the average customer waits in line for 1 minute, then waits at the cash register for 30 seconds while the cashier adds the cost of the items, and finally pays at the cash register for 30 more seconds. <u>How many minutes does it take the average customer to check out</u>?

Circle the correct answer: 150 seconds   120 seconds   2 minutes   3 minutes

Step 1: Underline the question that you will need to answer.

Step 2: List the facts (label each number).

Facts	Facts With Same Unit of Measure
1 minute 30 seconds 30 seconds	60 seconds waiting in line 30 seconds while the cashier adds the cost 30 seconds while the customer pays

There is a fact in this word problem that you <u>don't</u> need to know in order to find the answer. What is it?

I don't need to know that the manager timed 100 customers to figure out the average amount of time.

Step 3: Write a math sentence. Label your answer.

60 seconds + 30 seconds + 30 seconds = 120 seconds

120 seconds is the time it takes for the average customer to check out. The underlined part of the word problem says, "How many MINUTES does it take the average customer to check out?" I need to change 120 seconds to <u>2 minutes</u>. 2 minutes is the answer.

Step 4: Check your answer.

I answered the question I underlined, and the answer is in <u>minutes</u>.

Common Mistake

Sometimes, kids do not carefully read the underlined sentence. The question asks how many <u>minutes</u> it takes the average customer to check out. Some kids figure out the number of seconds correctly, and then answer 120 seconds. Even though 120 seconds is the same as 2 minutes, you need to give your answer in minutes.

If you did not answer the problem correctly, try again.

© 2013 The Critical Thinking Co.™ • www.CriticalThinking.com • 800-458-4849

Exercise 7

Three frogs named Benny, Ella, and Duke are competing for the title of Farthest Jumper. Benny jumps $1\frac{1}{2}$ meters. Ella jumps 100 centimeters more than Benny. But Duke jumps the farthest, jumping 50 centimeters more than Ella. How far did Duke jump?

(hint: 1 meter = 100 centimeters)

Circle the correct answer: $2\frac{1}{2}$ meters   3 meters $3\frac{1}{2}$ meters   4 meters

Stuck? Write labels for all the numbers. Still stuck? Please turn the page for the solution.

Solution

Three frogs named Benny, Ella, and Duke are competing for the title of Farthest Jumper. Benny jumps $1\frac{1}{2}$ meters. Ella jumps 100 centimeters more than Benny. But Duke Jumps the farthest, jumping 50 centimeters more than Ella. <u>How far did Duke jump</u>? (1 meter = 100 centimeters)

Circle the correct answer: $2\frac{1}{2}$ meters   ⬭ 3 meters $3\frac{1}{2}$ meters   4 meters

Step 1: Underline the question that you will need to answer.

Step 2: List the facts (label each number).

Facts	Facts With Same Unit of Measure
Benny jumps $1\frac{1}{2}$ meters Ella jumps 100 centimeters more than Benny Duke jumps 50 centimeters more than Ella	Benny jumps $1\frac{1}{2}$ meters Ella jumps 1 meter more than Benny Duke jumps $\frac{1}{2}$ meter more than Ella

Another way to solve this problem is to change all the units of measure to centimeters. If I'm working with centimeters, then Benny jumps 150 centimeters, Ella jumps 100 centimeters more than Benny, and Duke jumps 50 centimeters more than Ella.

Step 3: Write a math sentence. Label your answer.

Meters
$1\frac{1}{2}$ meters that Benny jumped
+ 1 meter more that Ella jumped
+ $\frac{1}{2}$ meter more that Duke jumped
3 meters ← <u>length that Duke jumped</u>

Centimeters
150 centimeters that Benny jumped
100 centimeters more that Ella jumped
50 centimeters more that Duke jumped
300 centimeters ← <u>length that Duke jumped</u>

If I work with centimeters, I have to change the answer back to meters:
300 centimeters = 3 meters ← the length that Duke jumped

Step 4: Check your answer.

I answered the question I underlined, and the answer is in <u>meters</u>.

Common Mistakes

- Sometimes students are not sure whether to change the units of measure to meters or to centimeters. However, the problem can be solved either way, although the answer must be in meters.

- Sometimes students don't see that they have to add all of the distances to get the length that Duke jumped.

If you did not answer the problem correctly, try again.

© 2013 The Critical Thinking Co.™ • www.CriticalThinking.com • 800-458-4849

Exercise 8

At the Emerson school, the 3rd, 4th, and 5th graders are collecting pennies to raise money for an animal shelter.

The 3rd graders collected so many pennies that they filled 2 gallon jars.
The 4th graders collected enough pennies to fill 3 quart jars.
The 5th graders collected enough pennies to fill a 1 gallon jar and a 1 quart jar.

How many quart jars of pennies did the students collect in all?
(hint: 1 gallon jar = 4 quart jars)

Circle the correct answer: 3 gallon jars   6 quart jars   11 quart jars   16 quart jars

Stuck? Write labels for all the numbers. Still stuck? Please turn the page for the solution.

Solution

At the Emerson school, the 3rd, 4th, and 5th graders are collecting pennies to raise money for an animal shelter.

The 3rd graders collected so many pennies that they filled 2 gallon jars.
The 4th graders collected enough pennies to fill 3 quart jars.
The 5th graders collected enough pennies to fill a 1 gallon jar and a 1 quart jar.

<u>How many quart jars of pennies did the students collect in all</u>? (hint: 1 gallon jar = 4 quart jars)

Circle the correct answer: 3 gallon jars   6 quart jars   11 quart jars   (16 quart jars)

Step 1: Underline the question that you will need to answer.

Step 2:   List the facts (label each number).

Facts	(Multiplication)	Facts With Same Unit of Measure
2 gallon jars 3 quart jars 1 gallon jar and 1 quart jar	2 x 4 = 8	8 quart jars collected by the 3rd graders 3 quart jars collected by the 4th graders 1 gallon jar = 4 quart jars + 1 quart jar 5 quart jars collected by the 5th graders

Step 3: Write a math sentence. Label your answer.

8 + 3 + 5 = 16 ← the number of quart jars that all the students collected

Step 4: Check your answer.

I answered the question I underlined, and the answer is in <u>quart jars</u>, which is the correct unit of measure.

Common Mistake

The unit of measure is "quart jars" and there are 4 quart jars in every gallon. Some students get confused when they see that the 5th graders collected 1 gallon and 1 quart jar. It gets easier when they understand that the 5th graders collected 5 quart jars.

If you did not answer the problem correctly, then try again.

© 2013 The Critical Thinking Co.™ • www.CriticalThinking.com • 800-458-4849

XI. Estimation in Word Problems

Believe it or not, there are times on a test when you should NOT figure out the exact answers. On a test, there are word problems that ask you to estimate **about** how much someone has or needs.

Whenever a test question asks you to find **about** how much, you need to use **estimation** in order to find the correct answer.

> Usually, when you estimate, you should round the number so that you work with **1** digit.

For example, if you have the number 729, you would usually round the number to the nearest hundred, so that you would work with the number 700, which has only 1 digit that you would need to work with. You do not need to work with 0s.

729 → 700

> "Now I can work with only 1 digit. It will be easier to write a math sentence and figure out the answer."

> However, if you want a **closer, more accurate** estimate (an estimate that is closer to the exact answer), you can round the number so that you work with **2** digits.

If you have the number 729, and want a more accurate estimate, you can round the number to the nearest 10, so that you would work with the number 730.

729 → 730

> "Now I have to work with 2 digits. It will take more time to write a math sentence and figure out the answer, but my answer will be more accurate (closer to the exact answer)."

> Here's the cool thing about estimation: Whether you round the number so that you work with 1 digit or with 2 or more digits, you are not wrong.

© 2013 The Critical Thinking Co.™ • www.CriticalThinking.com • 800-458-4849

Guided Practice

These next problems **do not** ask you to figure out exact answers. Instead, they ask you to **estimate** answers. These estimation problems can be answered using the same strategies that you already know.

Before you write your number sentence, you will have to **change the numbers in your fact list to estimates**.

Most of the time, you will round the numbers in your fact list so that you will work with only 1 digit.

Sometimes, if you want to estimate in a way that is more accurate (closer to the real answer), you can round numbers so that you work with 2 digits.

With practice, you will get better at deciding whether to use 1 or 2 digit estimates.

After each of these estimation problems, you can check your work by looking at the solution.

© 2013 The Critical Thinking Co.™ • www.CriticalThinking.com • 800-458-4849

Exercise 1

Every year at the London Zoo, the zookeepers count all the animals. This past year, the zookeepers counted 183 mammals and 104 birds and amphibians. About how many animals were at the London Zoo? (hint: round to the nearest hundred)

Circle the correct answer: 100   200   300   400

Step 1: Underline the question that you will need to answer.

Step 2: List the facts (label each number).

Facts	Facts With Rounded Numbers
_____	_____
_____	_____

Step 3: Write a math sentence. Label your answer.

Step 4: Check your answer.

Stuck? Write labels for all the numbers. Still stuck? Please turn the page for the solution.

© 2013 The Critical Thinking Co.™ • www.CriticalThinking.com • 800-458-4849

Solution

Every year at the London Zoo, the zookeepers count all the animals. This past year, the zookeepers counted 183 mammals and 104 birds and amphibians. <u>About how many animals were at the London Zoo</u>? (hint: round to the nearest hundred)

Circle the correct answer: 100   200   ⟨300⟩   400

Step 1: Underline the question that you will need to answer.

Step 2: List the facts (label each number).

Facts	Facts With Rounded Numbers
183	183 → 200 mammals
104	104 → 100 birds and amphibians

Step 3: Write a math sentence. Label your answer.

200 + 100 = about 300 animals

Step 4: Check your answer.

My answer makes sense.

If you did not answer the problem correctly, try again.

© 2013 The Critical Thinking Co.™ • www.CriticalThinking.com • 800-458-4849

Exercise 2

Ava decided that she wanted an even better estimate of the number of animals at the London Zoo than the one that was given in the last problem. She decided to round the numbers to the nearest **ten** before she wrote her math sentence. Using Ava's more accurate estimate, about how many animals were at the London Zoo?

This past year, the zookeepers counted 183 mammals and 104 birds and amphibians (round to the nearest 10).

Circle the correct answer: 280   290   300   310

Step 1: Underline the question that you will need to answer.

Step 2: List the facts (label each number).

Facts	Facts With Rounded Numbers
_____	_____
_____	_____

Step 3: Write a math sentence. Label your answer.

Step 4: Check your answer.

Stuck? Write labels for all the numbers. Still stuck? Please turn the page for the solution.

Solution

Ava decided that she wanted an even better estimate of the number of animals at the London Zoo than the one that was given in the last problem. She decided to round the numbers to the nearest **ten** before she wrote her math sentence. Using Ava's more accurate estimate, about how many animals were at the London Zoo?

This past year, the zookeepers counted 183 mammals and 104 birds and amphibians (round to the nearest 10).

Circle the correct answer: 280   290   300   310

Step 1: Underline the question that you will need to answer.

Step 2: List the facts (label each number).

Facts	Facts With Rounded Numbers
183 104	183 → 180 mammals 104 → 100 birds and amphibians

Step 3: Write a math sentence. Label your answer.

180 + 100 = about 280 animals

Step 4: Check your answer.

My answer makes sense.

If you did not answer the problem correctly, try again.

 © 2013 The Critical Thinking Co.™ • www.CriticalThinking.com • 800-458-4849

Exercise 3

Tony is reading a challenging 300 page book. He has read 25 pages. He has only 12 pages to go before he finishes the first chapter. Tony thinks, "Wow, I'll have read about 50 pages when I'm done with the first chapter!" Is Tony right?

Circle the correct answer.
   a. Tony is right. He will have read about 50 pages.
   b. Tony is wrong. He will have read about 30 pages.
   c. Tony is wrong. He will have read about 40 pages.
   d. Tony is wrong. He will have read about 60 pages.

Step 1: Underline the question that you will need to answer.

Step 2: List the facts (label each number).

Facts	Facts With Rounded Numbers
_____	_____
_____	_____

There is a fact in this word problem that you <u>don't</u> need to know in order to find the answer. What is it?

_____

_____

Step 3: Write a math sentence. Label your answer.

Step 4: Check your answer.

Stuck? Write labels for all the numbers. Still stuck? Please turn the page for the solution.

Solution

Tony is reading a challenging 300 page book. He has read 25 pages. He has only 12 pages to go before he finishes the first chapter. Tony thinks, "<u>Wow, I'll have read about 50 pages when I'm done with the first chapter!</u>" <u>Is Tony right</u>?

Circle the correct answer.
  a. Tony is right. He will have read about 50 pages.
  b. Tony is wrong. He will have read about 30 pages.
  (c.) Tony is wrong. He will have read about 40 pages.
  d. Tony is wrong. He will have read about 60 pages.

Step 1: Underline the question that you will need to answer.

Step 2: List the facts (label each number).

Facts	Facts With Rounded Numbers
25 12	25 → 30 pages Tony has read 12 → 10 pages to go before he finishes the first chapter

There is a fact in this word problem that you <u>don't</u> need to know in order to find the answer. What is it?

I don't need to know that the book has 300 pages.

Step 3: Write a math sentence. Label your answer.

30 + 10 = about 40 pages that Tony will have read

Step 4: Check your answer.

My answer makes sense.

If you did not answer the problem correctly, try again.

© 2013 The Critical Thinking Co.™ • www.CriticalThinking.com • 800-458-4849

The steps will not be included in the next exercises, except in the solutions.

Exercise 4

Mr. Bean has an appointment to see the dentist at 2:30. It will take him 50 minutes to get from his house to the dentist's office. He can be early, and wait in the waiting room. However, he cannot be late. About what time should Mr. Bean leave his house?

Circle the correct answer: 1:00   1:30   1:45   2:00

Stuck? Write labels for all the numbers. Still stuck? Please turn the page for the solution.

Solution

Mr. Bean has an appointment to see the dentist at 2:30. It will take him 50 minutes to get from his house to the dentist's office. He can be early, and wait in the waiting room. However, he cannot be late. <u>About what time should Mr. Bean leave his house</u>?

Circle the correct answer: 1:00 (1:30) 1:45 2:00

Step 1: Underline the question that you will need to answer.

Step 2: List the facts (label each number).

Facts	Facts With Rounded Numbers
2:30 50 minutes	2:30 ← the time that he needs to be at the dentist's office about 1 hour ← the time it will take for him to get to the dentist's office

I have to think about what numbers I should round. It makes sense to round 50 minutes to one hour. However, it does not make sense to round off the time of the appointment, which is 2:30.

Step 3: Write a math sentence. Label your answer.

2:30 – 1 hour = 1:30 ← the time that Mr. Bean should leave his house

Step 4: Check your answer.

My answer makes sense.

Common Mistakes

- Some students believe that the time of the appointment, 2:30, should be changed into a rounded number. However, not every number in an estimation problem should be rounded. This is a very good example of a number that should not be rounded.

- This problem involves more common sense than math. If Mr. Bean leaves at 1:30, he probably will get to the dentist about 10 minutes early. If he leaves at 1:00, he will be there on time, but he will be about 40 minutes early. It makes sense that 1:30 is the best answer. The last two answer choices cannot be correct because he will be late for the appointment if he leaves at 1:45 or 2:00.

If you did not answer the problem correctly, try again.

© 2013 The Critical Thinking Co.™ • www.CriticalThinking.com • 800-458-4849

Exercise 5

Spencer went to the store to buy art supplies. Here is a list of the prices of all the things that Spencer put in the shopping cart:

- $2.69 markers
- $1.98 glue
- $2.89 poster board

About how much money will Spencer need in order to pay for the art supplies?

Circle the correct answer: $6.00 $7.00 $8.00 $9.00

Stuck? Write labels for all the numbers. Still stuck? Please turn the page for the solution.

Solution

Spencer went to the store to buy art supplies. Here is a list of the prices of all the things that Spencer put in the shopping cart:

- $2.69 markers
- $1.98 glue
- $2.89 poster board

<u>About how much money will Spencer need in order to pay for the art supplies</u>?

Circle the correct answer: $6.00 $7.00 $8.00 $9.00

Step 1: Underline the question that you will need to answer.

Step 2: List the facts (label each number).

Facts	Facts With Rounded Numbers
$2.69	$2.69 → $3.00 markers
$1.98	$1.98 → $2.00 glue
$2.89	$2.89 → $3.00 poster board

Step 3: Write a math sentence. Label your answer.

$3.00 + $2.00 + 3.00 = $8.00 that Spencer will pay for the art supplies

Step 4: Check your answer.

My answer makes sense.

Common Mistake

Some students might be uncomfortable rounding the cost of the markers, which is $2.69, all the way up to $3.00. However, in looking over the answer choices, it seems that it is not necessary to be more accurate. Rounding to one digit (the nearest dollar) is still okay. If one of the answer choices were $7.50, this would be a more difficult problem. So $8.00 is a good estimate, even though rounding to 2 digits would give an estimate that is closer to the actual cost.

If you did not answer the problem correctly, try again.

Congratulations! You have learned how to estimate the answer to word problems. If you didn't get a problem right the first time and then tried it a second time, you should be very proud of yourself for trying again. Remember, good students don't always answer all the questions correctly, but they stick with it and try again.

If you would like to practice with more difficult word problems, you can go on to Advanced Guided Practice. However, if you would like to stop here, that is fine.

© 2013 The Critical Thinking Co.™ • www.CriticalThinking.com • 800-458-4849

Advanced Guided Practice

Exercise 6

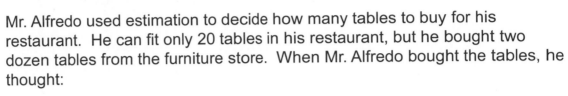

Mr. Alfredo wants to open a restaurant. He can fit 20 tables in his restaurant. He buys 2 dozen tables from a furniture store. (hint: 1 dozen = 12)

   a. Write the **exact number** of tables that Mr. Alfredo bought. _____

Mr. Alfredo used estimation to decide how many tables to buy for his restaurant. He can fit only 20 tables in his restaurant, but he bought two dozen tables from the furniture store. When Mr. Alfredo bought the tables, he thought:

"I should buy 2 dozen tables. If I round one dozen, then that means that each dozen is about 10. Two groups of 10 is 20. That's perfect! All the tables will fit in my restaurant!"

b. Was it a good idea for Mr. Alfredo to have used the estimate of 20 when he bought tables for his restaurant? Why or why not?
   (hint: Remember to restate the question, and use specific information in your answer.)

_____

_____

_____

_____

> Stuck? Write labels for all the numbers. Still stuck? Please turn the page for the solution.

© 2013 The Critical Thinking Co.™ • www.CriticalThinking.com • 800-458-4849

Solution

Mr. Alfredo wants to open a restaurant. He can fit 20 tables in his restaurant. He buys 2 dozen tables from a furniture store. (hint: 1 dozen = 12)

a. Write the **exact number** of tables that Mr. Alfredo bought. _____24_____

Step 1: Underline the question that you will need to answer.

Step 2: List the facts (label each number).

2 dozen tables (1 dozen = 12)

Step 3: Write a math sentence. Label your answer.

2 × 12 = 24 ← the exact number of tables that Mr. Alfredo bought

Step 4: Check your answer.

My answer makes sense.

Mr. Alfredo used estimation to decide how many tables to buy for his restaurant. He can fit only 20 tables in his restaurant, but he bought two dozen tables from the furniture store. When Mr. Alfredo bought the tables, he thought:

"I should buy 2 dozen tables. If I round one dozen, then that means that each dozen is about 10. Two groups of 10 is 20. That's perfect! All the tables will fit in my restaurant!"

b. Was it a good idea for Mr. Alfredo to have used the estimate of 20 when he bought tables for his restaurant? Why or why not?

(hint: Remember to restate the question, and use specific information from the passage in your answer.)

It was not a good idea for Mr. Alfredo to have used the estimate of 20 when he bought tables for his restaurant. He estimated that he bought 20 tables, but he really bought 24. 24 tables will not fit in his restaurant.

If you did not answer the problem correctly, then try again.

© 2013 The Critical Thinking Co.™ • www.CriticalThinking.com • 800-458-4849

Exercise 7

Ms. Brag sold 507 hot dogs from her hot dog stand. She knew that Mr. Mellow had sold only 394 hot dogs from his stand. Ms. Brag loudly announced, "I've sold about 200 more hot dogs than you, Mr. Mellow!" Use estimation to show whether or not Ms. Brag is correct, and then explain why Ms. Brag is or is not correct.

_____

_____

_____

_____

_____

Stuck? Write labels for all the numbers. Still stuck? Please turn the page for the solution.

Solution

Ms. Brag sold 507 hot dogs from her hot dog stand. She knew that Mr. Mellow had sold only 394 hot dogs from his stand. Ms. Brag loudly announced, "I've sold about 200 more hot dogs than you, Mr. Mellow!" <u>Use estimation to show whether or not Ms. Brag is correct, and then explain why Ms. Brag is or is not correct.</u>

Using estimation, I found that Ms. Brag is not correct. Ms. Brag sold about 500 hot dogs, and Mr. Mellow sold about 400 hot dogs. Ms. Brag sold about 100 more hot dogs than Mr. Mellow. Ms. Brag says that she sold about 200 more hot dogs than Mr. Mellow. This cannot be correct, because 200 is much higher than the estimate of 100.

Step 1: Underline the question that you will need to answer.

Step 2: List the facts (label each number).

Facts	Facts With Rounded Numbers
507	507 → 500 hot dogs sold by Ms. Brag
394	394 → 400 hot dogs sold by Mr. Mellow

200 more is the number of hot dogs that Ms. Brag thinks she sold when she compares her sales to Mr. Mellow's.

Step 3: Write a math sentence. Label your answer.

500 - 400 = 100 ← This is about how many more hot dogs Ms. Brag sold.

Step 4: Check your answer.

My answer makes sense.

If you did not answer the problem correctly, try again.

© 2013 The Critical Thinking Co.™ • www.CriticalThinking.com • 800-458-4849

Exercise 8

The World's Tallest Buildings

Height (in feet)	Name of Building	Location
2,723	Burj Khalifa	Dubai, United Arab Emirates
1,969	Canton Tower	Guangzhou, China
1,814	CN Tower	Toronto, Canada

After looking at the chart above, Emory wondered, "If these buildings were stacked on top of each other, how tall would the structure be?" Circle the best estimate of the answer to Emory's question.

Circle the correct answer: 6,000 feet   6,500 feet   6,750 feet   7,250 feet

Stuck? Write labels for all the numbers. Still stuck? Please turn the page for the solution.

Solution

After looking at the chart above, Emory wondered, "<u>How many feet tall would it be if</u> <u>these three buildings were piled one on top of the other</u>?" <u>Circle the best estimate of</u> <u>the answer to Emory's question</u>.

Circle the correct answer: 6,000 feet   ⬭6,500 feet⬭   6,750 feet   7,250 feet

Step 1: Underline the question that you will need to answer.

Step 2: List the facts (label each number).

Facts	Facts With Rounded Numbers	
height in feet	nearest hundred	nearest thousand
2,723 →	2,700	3,000
1,969 →	2,000	2,000
1,814 →	1,800	2,000
Sum	6,500 feet	7,000 feet

Step 3: Write a math sentence. Label your answer.

When I add all the numbers that were rounded to the nearest hundred, I get 6,500 as my estimate.

But when I add all the numbers that were rounded to the nearest thousand, I get 7,000 as my estimate.

Step 4: Check your answer.

When I look at the answer choices, I know that I should use the estimate that came from rounding to the nearest hundred, which is 6,500 feet.

If you did not answer the problem correctly, try again.

© 2013 The Critical Thinking Co.™ • www.CriticalThinking.com • 800-458-4849

XII. Understand Charts

Charts show you information that is called **data**. **Data** are *facts*. When you look at data in a chart, you can learn a lot about something in a short time.

Here are some types of charts that you might see on a test:

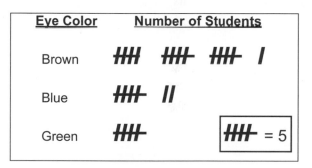

Day	Visitors at the Park
Saturday	360
Sunday	290
Monday	100

Table

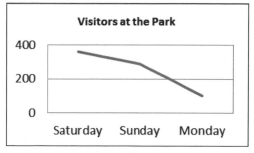

Line Graph

Tally Chart

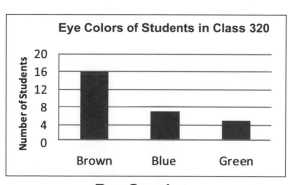

Bar Graph

Pie Chart

Pictograph

© 2013 The Critical Thinking Co.™ • www.CriticalThinking.com • 800-458-4849

Sometimes, two *different* charts can be used to show the same data.

For example, the **table** with the title *Visitors at the Park* shows the same data as the **line graph**, *Visitors at the Park*.

1. Look at the kinds of charts shown on the previous page. Which other two charts show the same data?
   a. the tally chart and the bar graph
   b. the Eye Color and the Students
   c. the pie chart and the pictograph
   d. the line graph and the bar graph

What is the difference between a **chart** and a **graph**?

A chart shows data in a list (like a table). A graph almost always shows data as a picture. Whether it's called a chart or a graph, <u>the way that you understand the data is the same</u>.

© 2013 The Critical Thinking Co.™ • www.CriticalThinking.com • 800-458-4849

Parts of a Chart

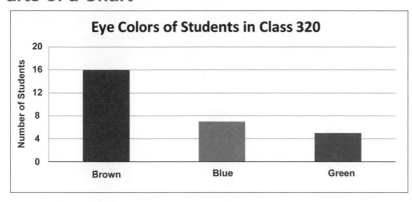

The three basic parts of all charts are:

1. The Title

The title is the easiest part of a chart to understand. The title tells you what the chart is about. Most charts have titles.

Take a look at the bar graph above. The **title** is *Eye Colors of Students in Class 320*.

2. The Labels

All charts and graphs have labels. To understand what the chart means, it must have labels.

For the bar graph above, the **labels** are *Number of Students* and three different eye colors: *Brown*, *Blue*, and *Green*.

3. The Scale

The scale shows numbers and tells you how much there is of something. Understanding the scale can be tricky. Sometimes, you may have to estimate when you read a chart because the scale is not always exact.

For the bar graph above, the **scale** is shown along the label *Number of Students*. Each line represents 4 students. However, look at the label *Green* in the bar graph. There are not exactly 4 students with green eyes. You will have to estimate how many students have green eyes.

2. Circle the best estimate of the number of students with green eyes.
    a. 4
    b. 5
    c. 7
    d. 8

In the Guided Practice, you will be looking at data shown in charts and graphs. As you answer the questions, remember to:

1. Think about the <u>labels</u> and what they represent. When you understand the labels, you will understand the chart.

2. Pay attention to the <u>scale</u>, and make sure you know the amount that each notch on the scale represents.

3. Read the chart as well as you can, and <u>make a good estimate</u> when the scale is not very accurate.

Guided Practice

Exercise 1

A new museum opened in January. The line graph below shows the number of visitors at the museum over the past 6 months.

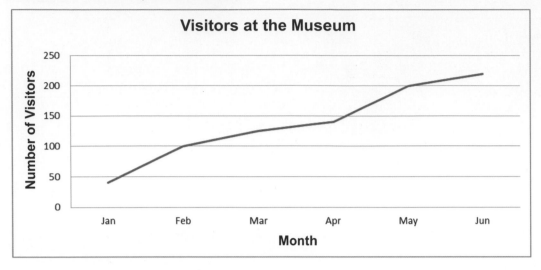

3. Write the <u>title</u> of the line graph.

_____

4. Write the <u>labels</u>.

_____

_____

5. Which statement best describes the <u>scale</u>?
   a. The scale shows one line for every visitor.
   b. The scale shows one line for every 100 visitors.
   c. The scale shows one line for every 50 visitors.
   d. The scale shows two lines for every 10 visitors.

6. About how many people visited the museum in February?
   a. 100
   b. 125
   c. 150
   d. 200

7. Which question can be answered by looking at the line graph?
   a. How many people visited the museum each month?
   b. How many people visited the museum on Sunday?
   c. Did people enjoy their visit at the museum?
   d. Should we build a new exhibit at the museum?

© 2013 The Critical Thinking Co.™ • www.CriticalThinking.com • 800-458-4849

Exercise 2

Isaac took a survey of his classmates. He asked them to vote for their favorite activity to do after school. The tally chart below shows the results of Isaac's survey.

Activity	Basketball	Soccer	Drama	Karate
Number of Votes	ℍℍ I	ℍℍ	ℍℍ II	III

ℍℍ = 5

8. Isaac decided to make a bar graph. Which bar graph shows the results correctly? _____

a.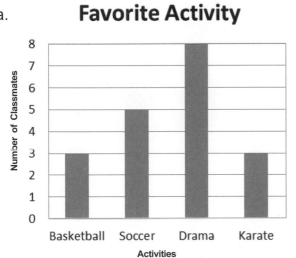

b.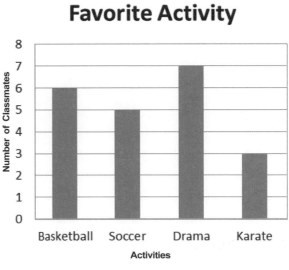

c.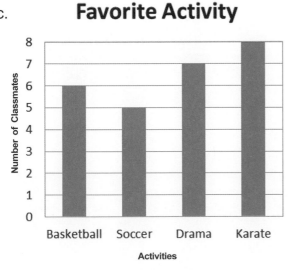

d.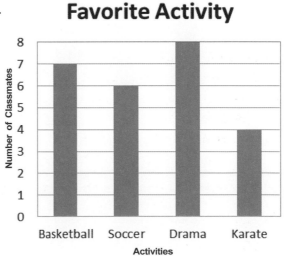

9. What is something that Isaac could say about the results?
   a. There were 10 kids who took the survey.
   b. Drama is the favorite after school activity.
   c. Basketball is the favorite after school activity.
   d. Ten kids voted that soccer was their favorite after school activity.

© 2013 The Critical Thinking Co.™ • www.CriticalThinking.com • 800-458-4849

Exercise 3

At a carnival, Luke, Jared, and Alicia played games and earned tickets for every game that they won. The tickets were different colors, and each color was worth a different number of points. Below is a chart showing each ticket and how many points it was worth.

red ticket = 10 points

blue ticket = 5 points

yellow ticket = 2 points

At the end of the day, Luke, Jared, and Alicia counted their tickets. Here is a chart showing the tickets that each of the friends won.

Luke

Jared

Alicia

10. Who has the most <u>tickets</u>?
- a. Luke
- b. Jared
- c. Alicia
- d. a tie between Luke and Alicia

11. Who has the most <u>points</u>? (hint: You may have to write math sentences to find the answer.)
- a. Luke
- b. Jared
- c. Alicia
- d. a tie between Luke and Jared

© 2013 The Critical Thinking Co.™ • www.CriticalThinking.com • 800-458-4849

Exercise 4

Three different classes at the Brookdale School visited a flower garden. Each class was asked to count the number of tulips they saw. The pictograph below shows the results.

Mr. Walker's class

Ms. O'Shea's class

Ms. Zuniga's class

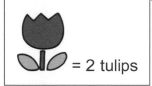
= 2 tulips

12. Which question can be answered by looking at the pictograph?
   a. What is the favorite flower of the students in Ms. O'Shea's class?
   b. Which class liked the garden the most?
   c. Which class counted the most tulips?
   d. Which class correctly counted the number of tulips they saw?

13. How many tulips did Ms. Zuniga's class count?
   a. 4
   b. 4½
   c. 8½
   d. 9

Congratulations! You have learned how to think carefully about charts and graphs. Check your answers in the Answer Key on page 217.

If you would like to practice with more difficult questions, you can go on to Advanced Guided Practice. However, if you would like to stop here, that is fine.

© 2013 The Critical Thinking Co.™ • www.CriticalThinking.com • 800-458-4849

Advanced Guided Practice

Exercise 5 ——————————————————————————

A petting zoo was starting a new program where kids could spend the day taking care of a pet.

The owner of the petting zoo wanted to know what kinds of pets should be used in the program. The owner thought that younger kids and older kids would like to take care of different types of pets.

The owner gave the two groups of kids a survey. In one group there were younger kids (ages 4-7). In the second group, there were older kids (ages 8-11). You can see the survey below.

This is the question that the students were asked:

> If you could spend a day taking care of any of these four pets, which one would you choose?
>
> circle one: horse   cat   dog   hamster

The results of the survey are shown in the bar graph below:

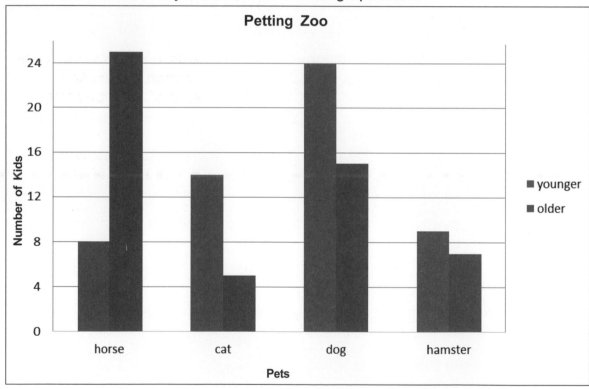

14. About how many of the younger kids chose a cat?
   a. 5
   b. 12
   c. 13
   d. 14

© 2013 The Critical Thinking Co.™ • www.CriticalThinking.com • 800-458-4849

15. Fifty-two older kids were given the survey. Which pet received about **half** of the votes from the older kids?
    a. horse
    b. cat
    c. dog
    d. hamster

16. Which pet got the **fewest** votes from the younger and older kids **combined**?
    a. horse
    b. cat
    c. dog
    d. hamster

17. Based on the bar graph, which of the following statements is true?
    a. A dog was chosen equally as often by the younger and older kids.
    b. Most of the older kids chose a dog.
    c. Most of the younger kids chose a cat.
    d. Among the older kids, a dog was chosen about twice as often as a hamster.

18. What is the best conclusion to be drawn from the survey?
    a. Younger kids like to take care of common pets like cats, dogs, and hamsters. Older kids would like to try to take care of pets that are not as common, like horses.
    b. Younger kids are scared of horses. Older kids are not scared of any type of pet.
    c. Younger kids own cats, dogs, and hamsters more often than older kids, but older kids own horses more often than younger kids.
    d. Younger kids like to take care of all kinds of pets and have no clear favorite, but older kids clearly prefer to take care of dogs more than any other type of pet.

Exercise 6

The populations of two towns that are next to one another, the towns of Apple Valley and Sugar Hill, are shown in the line graph below.

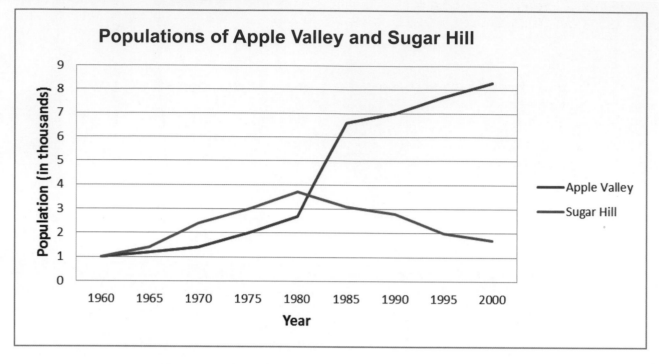

Populations of Apple Valley and Sugar Hill

19. What is the best estimate of the population of Apple Valley in 1985?
    a. 6,500
    b. 8,500
    c. 65,000
    d. 85,000

20. Apple Valley is home to a very successful pie company called Best Apple Pie. Best Apple Pie moved to Apple Valley in 1980.

    Do you think that Best Apple Pie changed the populations of Apple Valley and Sugar Hill? Use the data in the line graph to support your answer.

    _____

    _____

    _____

    _____

© 2013 The Critical Thinking Co.™ • www.CriticalThinking.com • 800-458-4849

If you have not studied percentages yet, then skip questions 21 and 22 for now.

Exercise 7

Ms. Shaw owns an ice cream shop. She asked people in her shop to name their favorite ice cream flavor. She made the pie chart below to show the results.

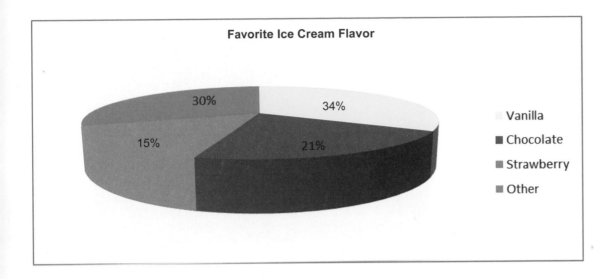

Favorite Ice Cream Flavor

- Vanilla
- Chocolate
- Strawberry
- Other

21. What question can be answered from the data shown in the pie chart?
    a. How many different ice cream flavors did people name when they chose "Other" instead of "Vanilla," "Chocolate," or "Strawberry"?
    b. What flavor of ice cream do most people say is their favorite?
    c. How many people say that strawberry is their favorite ice cream flavor?
    d. How many people say that they do not like ice cream at all?

22. Let's say that Ms. Shaw surveyed 100 people. Now what can you say about the pie chart that you could NOT say before?
    a. People prefer chocolate more often than strawberry.
    b. People prefer vanilla more than any other flavor of ice cream.
    c. Fifteen people said that strawberry was their favorite ice cream flavor.
    d. When people chose "Other" instead of "Vanilla," "Chocolate," or "Strawberry," they named 22 different flavors.

© 2013 The Critical Thinking Co.™ • www.CriticalThinking.com • 800-458-4849

XIII. Understand Patterns

A **pattern** is a set of pictures or a set of numbers that follows a **rule**.

On most tests, there are questions that ask you to **predict** what comes next in a series of numbers or pictures. To answer these questions, it's important for you understand math patterns.

In this section, you will learn how to find a pattern's rule. Then you will learn how to use math to find out what comes next in the pattern.

Step 1: Find the pattern rule.

These are the basic rules for patterns:
   a. They can <u>repeat.</u>
   b. They can <u>increase.</u>
   c. They can <u>decrease.</u>
   d. They can follow more than one rule.

Exercise 1

Below is a simple **repeating** pattern that is shown with pictures.

_____

The **rule** for this pattern is first a dog, then a cat, and the pattern **repeats**.

Now that you know the rule, you can predict what comes next.

1. You know what comes next! Circle it.

Exercise 2

Below is a simple **increasing** pattern that is shown with numbers.

4, 6, 8, 10, 12, 14, _____

The rule for this pattern is that the numbers increase by 2.

Now that you know the rule, you can predict what comes next.

2. Circle the number that comes next.   13   15   16   18

© 2013 The Critical Thinking Co.™ • www.CriticalThinking.com • 800-458-4849

Exercise 3

Below is a simple **decreasing** pattern that is shown with pictures.

   _____

The rule for this pattern is that the oranges decrease by 1.

Now that you know the rule, you can predict what comes next.

3. Circle the number of oranges that will be next in the pattern.   4   3   2   1

Exercise 4

Sometimes, patterns can follow more than one rule.

The rule for the pattern below is that the numbers **increase** up to 3, and then **decrease** back down to 1.

1, 2, 3, 2, 1, 2, 3, 2, 1, 2, 3, _____

4. Circle the number that comes next in the pattern.   1   2   3   4

The rule for the pattern below is that the dog and cat **repeat**, but both animals also **increase** in size.

     _____

5. Circle what comes next:

Exercise 5

The rule for the pattern below is that the numbers **increase**, but the color also **repeats** between black and red.

1, 2, 3, 4, 5, 6, 7, 8, 9, 10, ____

6. Circle the number that comes next.   10   11   11   12

Exercise 6

Below is a pattern with a rule that is difficult to figure out, but it is easy when you know that the pattern follows two different rules.

First, let's look at the shapes. The rule for the shapes is that they repeat. There is a triangle, a square, and then a heart.

Second, let's look at the color. The rule for the color is that it repeats between black and red.

When you put **both** repeating patterns together, you have a pattern where the rule is that <u>the 3 shapes repeat, and the 2 colors also repeat</u>.

What comes next in the pattern seen above? Remember to think about the rule of both the shapes and the colors before you choose your answer.

7. Circle what comes next.   a. ■   b. ♥   c. ▲   d. ▲

© 2013 The Critical Thinking Co.™ • www.CriticalThinking.com • 800-458-4849

Exercise 7

Number patterns and picture patterns can follow the same rule.

The rule of this pattern is that every 3rd box is purple.

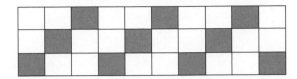

The rule of this pattern is that the numbers increase by 3.

3, 6, 9, 12, 15, 18, 21, 24, 27, 30

Let's put the picture pattern and the number pattern together.

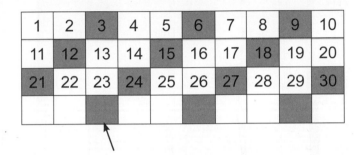

Every 3rd box is purple, and the numbers in the purple boxes increase by 3. The picture and number patterns follow the same rule.

8. See the arrow pointing to the purple box?

Circle the number that should be in that box. 31 32 33 34

Step 2: Use math to find what comes next.

Sometimes, you will need to add, subtract, multiply, or divide in order to find out what number comes next in the pattern.

Exercise 8

Use **addition** in order to find what number comes next in the pattern below.

1, 7, 13, 19, 25, 31, ____

If you're not sure what number comes next in the pattern, look at this drawing.

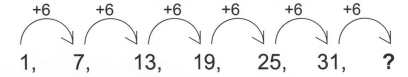

The number that comes next is <u>37</u>.

9. Circle the statement that best describes the rule for the above number pattern.
   a. The pattern <u>increases</u> by 6 each time. To figure out what comes next, add 6.
   b. The pattern <u>decreases</u> by 6 each time. To figure out what comes next, subtract 6.

Exercise 9

Use **subtraction** in order to find out what number comes next in the pattern below.

24, 20, 16, 12, ____

The pattern decreases by 4 each time. To figure out what number comes next, subtract 4.

10. Circle the number that comes next.   4   6   8   10

Exercise 10

Use **addition** in order to find out what number comes next in the pattern below. However, you need to **add a different number each time**.

$$1, 3, 6, 10, 15, 21, \underline{\hspace{1cm}}$$

If you're not sure what number comes next in the pattern, look at this drawing.

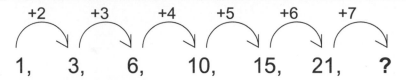

The number that comes next is <u>28</u>.

11. Circle the statement that best describes the rule for the above number pattern.
    a. The pattern increases by <u>one</u>. To figure out what comes next, add one.
    b. The pattern increases by <u>one more</u> each time. To figure out what comes next, add one more than you did the time before.
    c. The pattern increases by the <u>same number</u> each time, and that number is 6. To figure out what comes next, add 6.
    d. The pattern decreases by <u>one less</u> each time. To figure out what comes next, subtract and find one less than you did the time before.

Exercise 11

Use **multiplication** in order to find what number comes next in the pattern below.

$$2, 4, 8, 16$$

If you're not sure what number comes next in the pattern, look at this drawing.

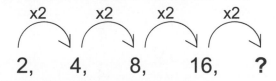

The number that comes next is <u>32</u>.

12. Circle the statement that best describes the rule for the above number pattern.
    a. The pattern <u>increases</u> so that each number is <u>2 times more</u> than the number before it.
    b. The pattern <u>decreases</u> so that each number is <u>2 times less</u> than the number before it.
    c. The pattern <u>increases</u> so that each number is <u>3 more</u> than the number before it.
    d. The pattern <u>decreases</u> so that each number is <u>2 less</u> than the number before it.

Exercise 12

Use **division** in order to find what number comes next in the pattern below.

$$243, 81, 27, 9, \underline{\quad}$$

The rule of the pattern is that it decreases. Each number in the pattern is divided by 3.

First $243 \div 3 = 81$, then $81 \div 3 = 27$, then $27 \div 3 = 9$. To figure out what comes next, divide by 3.

13. Circle the number that comes next.

27   9   3   1

© 2013 The Critical Thinking Co.™ • www.CriticalThinking.com • 800-458-4849

Guided Practice

In order to answer any question about a math pattern, follow these two steps:

Step 1: Find the pattern rule.

    a. Is the pattern repeating?
    b. Is the pattern increasing?
    c. Is the pattern decreasing?
    d. Is the pattern following more than one rule?

Step 2: Use math to find what comes next.

Add, subtract, multiply, or divide in order to find what number comes next in the pattern.

Not sure how to follow these two steps yet? Don't worry. You'll feel confident after you finish the Guided Practice.

Exercise 13

Look at the picture pattern below.

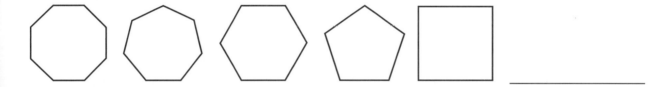

14. Circle the picture that should come next. (hint: Count the lines in each of the shapes.)

 a.   b.    c.   d.

15. State whether the pattern above is <u>repeating</u>, <u>increasing</u>, or <u>decreasing</u>.
(hint: Remember to write a complete sentence.)

_____

_____

16. Describe whether you need to <u>add</u> or <u>subtract</u> lines, and how many each time.

_____

_____

Exercise 14

Look at the picture pattern below.

1   3   5   7   _____

17. Circle what comes next in the number pattern below:

  1, 3, 5, 7, ____   8 9 10 11

18. Circle the picture that should come next:

 5   9   6   8

19. The number pattern (in problem 17, above) and the picture pattern (in problem 18, above) **follow the same rule**. What is the rule?
   a. The pattern is repeating.
   b. The pattern is increasing.
   c. The pattern is decreasing.

20. Describe the math you need to do in order to figure out what comes next.

_____

_____

© 2013 The Critical Thinking Co.™ • www.CriticalThinking.com • 800-458-4849

Exercise 15

Lionel plays soccer. He practices shooting the soccer ball in the goal. The bar graph below shows the number of times he shot the ball in the goal each day.

21.   Describe the pattern of how Lionel did from <u>Monday - Thursday</u>.

First, state whether his performance improved (like an increasing pattern), did not improve (like a decreasing pattern), or stayed the same (like a repeating pattern).

Then, state how many <u>more</u> goals he made each day.

_____

_____

_____

_____

© 2013 The Critical Thinking Co.™ • www.CriticalThinking.com • 800-458-4849

Now, take a look at Lionel's goal shooting practice from Thursday – Saturday.

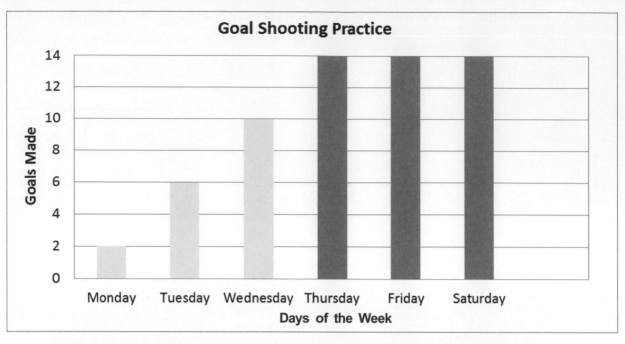

22. Describe the pattern of how Lionel did from <u>Thursday - Saturday</u>.

First, state whether his performance improved (like an increasing pattern), did not improve (like a decreasing pattern), or stayed the same (like a repeating pattern).

Then, state whether or not he made any additional goals each day.

_____

_____

_____

_____

23. If Lionel practiced on Sunday, how many goals would he probably make? Explain your answer.

_____

_____

_____

_____

Exercise 16

24. Look at the pattern below. Which picture should be in the blank space above the arrow (↑)?

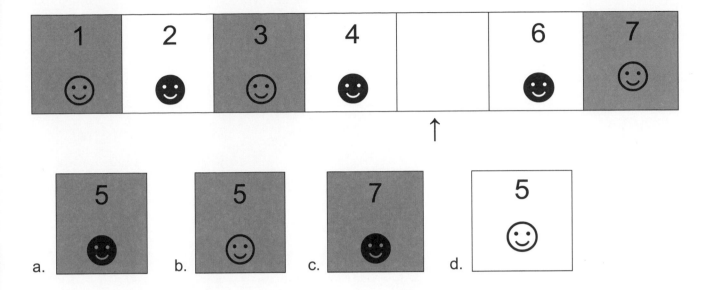

↑

a. 5 ☺

b. 5 ☺

c. 7 ☺

d. 5 ☺

Congratulations! You have learned how to do your best when you answer questions about math patterns. Check your answers in the Answer Key on page 218.

If you would like to practice with more difficult questions, you can go on to Advanced Guided Practice. However, if you would like to stop here, that is fine.

Advanced Guided Practice

Step 1: Find the pattern rule.

Step 2: Use math to find what comes next.

Exercise 17 ————————————————————————————

Look at the pattern below.

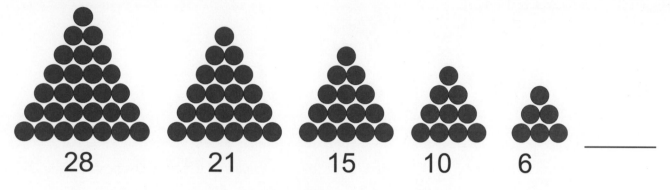

28   21   15   10   6   _____

25. Circle what comes next.

6   3   2   1

26. The picture pattern and the number pattern below it **follow the same rule**.
What is the rule? (hint: Describe the number of red balls in the bottom row and how it changes each time.)

_____

_____

_____

_____

© 2013 The Critical Thinking Co.™ • www.CriticalThinking.com • 800-458-4849

Exercise 18

27. Circle what will be the **12th** number in the pattern below.

7, 14, 21, 28, 21, 14, 7, 14, ___, ___, ___, ___

This is the space for the 12th number.

7   14   21   28

Exercise 19

Look at the pattern below.

0 2	3 4	6 6	3 8		3 12	6 14

↑

28. Which picture should be in the blank space above the arrow (↑)?

a. 0 10   b. 6 10   c. 6 9   d. 3 10

Exercise 20

Below is a menu that shows what a café served over the past four weeks.

Café Yum Yum — Closed weekends!

Monday	Tuesday	Wednesday	Thursday	Friday
Tacos	Chicken Nuggets	Make Your Own Salad	Macaroni and Cheese	Pizza
Chicken Nuggets	Make Your Own Salad	Macaroni and Cheese	Tacos	Pizza
Make Your Own Salad	Macaroni and Cheese	Tacos	Chicken Nuggets	Pizza
Macaroni and Cheese	Tacos	Chicken Nuggets	Make Your Own Salad	Pizza
		What will be served today?		What will be served today?

29. If the pattern continues, what will be served <u>next Friday</u>?
    a. Tacos
    b. Chicken Nuggets
    c. Make Your Own Salad
    d. Macaroni and Cheese
    e. Pizza

30. If the pattern continues, what will be served <u>next Wednesday</u>?
    a. Tacos
    b. Chicken Nuggets
    c. Make Your Own Salad
    d. Macaroni and Cheese
    e. Pizza

Exercise 21

31. A teacher started a website for the classroom pet, a cute baby hamster. The class made a table to count how many people had visited the website.

Visitors to the Website

Day	Visitors
Monday	2
Tuesday	4
Wednesday	8
Thursday	16
Friday	32

If the pattern in the table continues, how many people will have visited the website when the class meets again on Monday, after the weekend?

Circle the correct answer: 48   64   128   256

© 2013 The Critical Thinking Co.™ • www.CriticalThinking.com • 800-458-4849

XIV. Review

Use this review to show what you have learned from *Thinking Skills for Tests: Upper Elementary*.

Reading Skills for Tests

I. Vocabulary (page 1)

What does the word <u>vocabulary</u> mean?

Your vocabulary is all the words you know, and it grows when you try to figure out the meaning of words. Below are the steps you practiced in order to figure out the meaning of words on a test. **Try to remember these steps, because you will be asked about them on the next page.**

Step 1: Guess what the word means *before* you look at the answer choices.
Step 2: Try each answer choice in the sentence.
Step 3: Cross out the wrong answers.
Step 4: Choose the best answer.

To help you remember the steps, use them to figure out the meanings of the underlined word:

1. When you cross out answer choices that do not make sense, you <u>eliminate</u> the wrong answers.

Step 1: Guess what the word means *before* you look at the answer choices.

I think <u>eliminate</u> means _____

Step 2: Try each answer choice in the sentence.

a. keep
b. choose
c. get rid of
d. think about

Step 3: Cross out the wrong answers.

Step 4: Choose the best answer.

2. Below are the steps you reviewed on the last page. They are in the wrong order. Number the steps in the correct order.

_____ Choose the best answer.

_____ Cross out the wrong answers.

_____ Guess what the word means *before* you look at the answer choices.

_____ Try each answer choice in the sentence.

3. After you cross out wrong answers, you must then choose:
   a. the best answer.
   b. the correct answer.

This is a tricky question. You will not see tricky questions like this on a real test. This tricky question is here because it teaches you something. Go ahead and look at the Answer Key on page 218 to find out why this tricky question teaches you something important.

4. "When I take a test, do I always have to **write** what I think the word means before I look at the answer choices? Can't I just **think** about what the word might mean?"
   a. You must **write** what you think the word means before you look at the answer choices.
   b. In practice you wrote what you thought the word meant. However, after a while, even in practice, you were able to **think** about what the word meant without writing it down. As long as you guess what the word means <u>before</u> looking at the answer choices, even in thought, it will help you a lot!

© 2013 The Critical Thinking Co.™ • www.CriticalThinking.com • 800-458-4849

III. Answer Multiple Choice Questions (page 29)

You learned to read passages on tests in a way that is different from how you read when you are reading for fun. You also learned how to answer multiple choice questions about what you have read.

Below are the steps that you can use as you read and answer multiple choice questions on a test. **Try to remember these steps, because you will be asked about them on the next page.**

Step 1: Read the questions.
Step 2: Read the passage ONCE to understand the main idea. Underline important details.
Step 3: Reread only what will help you answer questions.
Step 4: Cross out the wrong answers, and then choose the best answer.

To help you remember the steps, use them as you read the passage below and answer a question.

When you take a test, you read **passages**. A passage is a short article, story, or poem. After you read a passage on a test, you answer questions about it. When you answer questions, you show what you have learned from reading the passage. If you are able to learn a lot from reading, then you have good **reading comprehension**. Sometimes, the part of a test where you read passages and answer questions about them is called "reading comprehension."

5. On a test, a passage is:
   a. the "reading comprehension" part of the test.
   b. a chapter.
   c. the part of the test that gives you instructions.
   d. a short article, story, or poem.

Step 1: Read the questions.

Step 2: Read the passage ONCE to understand the main idea. Underline important details.

Step 3: Reread only what will help you answer questions.

Step 4: Cross out the wrong answers, and then choose the best answer.

6. Below are the steps that you reviewed on the previous page. Write the words that belong in the blank spaces.
   a. Step 1: Read the _____.
   b. Step 2: Read the passage **once** to understand the main idea. _____ important details.
   c. Step 3: Reread only what will help you answer _____.
   d. Step 4: Cross out the wrong answers, and then choose the _____answer.

7. Reading the questions before you read a passage helps you to:
   a. underline what is important as you read.
   b. know what details might be important to reread later when you answer questions.
   c. read the passage without worrying about the details you may not understand right away.
   d. all of the above

8. The first time you read a passage on a test, you should read it only **once** in order to understand the main idea because:
   a. you will not waste time trying to understand every detail.
   b. you will understand the main idea first, and then reread to understand the details later that can help you answer questions.
   c. you will read mostly to understand the main idea, which is what is most important.
   d. all of the above

© 2013 The Critical Thinking Co.™ • www.CriticalThinking.com • 800-458-4849

IV. Give Written Answers (page 41)

When you give written answers about a passage, you do the same things you do when you read a passage and answer multiple choice questions.

Step 1: Read the questions.
Step 2: Read the passage ONCE to understand the main idea. Underline important details.
Step 3: Reread only what will help you answer questions.
Step 4: Write the answer in your own words.

However, Step 4 is different because you don't cross out wrong answers and then choose the best answer. You cannot! There are no answer choices!

Below is what you do in Step 4 when you give a written answer on a test. **Try to remember this step, because you will be asked about it on the next page**.

Step 4: Write the answer in your own words.
     a. Restate the question.
     b. Add information from the passage that describes the main idea. Be specific.
     c. Sometimes, state your own thoughts.

To help you remember this step, use it to answer a question about the passage below.

In the Answer Key (p. 213) for this book, you might have noticed that you were told that good students do not always get all the correct answers. That might seem a little strange, but the truth is, what makes you a good student is not that you always know the correct answers but that you keep trying to learn even when you get a wrong answer.

Something you might not know is that scientists have proven that what makes you a good student are those times when you find something difficult but you keep trying anyway. When students are given work that is difficult, the ones who keep trying to learn, even though it is difficult, are almost always the students who grow up to be successful people. So, the next time you think that something in school is difficult, remember, that is the time when you have a chance to keep trying and to show how good a student you really are.

9. What is the main idea of the passage?

    Step 4: Write the answer in your own words.
        a. Restate the question.

Start by restating the question:

"The main idea of the passage is that. . ." _____

_____

_____

    b. Add information from the passage that describes the main idea. Be specific.

_____

_____

    c. Sometimes, state your own thoughts.

_____

_____

State your own thoughts <u>only if</u> you think it will help you to explain your answer.

10. Below is Step 4 that you reviewed on the previous page. Write the important words that belong in the blank spaces.

    Step 4: Write the answer in your own words.
        a. Restate the _____.

        b. Add information from the _____that describes the main idea. Be specific.

        c. Sometimes, state your own _____.

© 2013 The Critical Thinking Co.™ • www.CriticalThinking.com • 800-458-4849

II. Understand the Main Idea (page 15) and VI. Infer Answers (page 71)

You learned how to understand the main idea when you read a passage on a test. You also learned how to infer answers that are not directly stated in the passage.

The next sentences are about understanding the main idea and inferring answers. They are also about what students think and feel while they read a passage on a test.

After each sentence, circle **T** if the sentence is **true**, or **F** if it is **false**.

11. I just read a passage on a test. I do not understand everything that I have just read. That means that I am not a good reader. **T F**

12. Good readers may not understand everything that they read in a passage on a test, but they always try to understand the main idea. **T F**

13. Even if I read a difficult passage with a lot of details I don't understand, I should still try to understand the main idea. **T F**

14. A passage can be one paragraph, or it can be many paragraphs. **T F**

15. Every paragraph has a main idea. **T F**

16. To figure out the main idea, I can ask myself, "What would be a good title for this paragraph or this passage?" **T F**

17. When I read a passage on a test, I should never pay attention to my own thoughts or feelings. I should only think about what is directly stated in the passage. **T F**

18. When you infer answers, you draw your own conclusions from clues in the passage. **T F**

19. The three main reasons authors write are to 1. inform, 2. tell a story, and 3. convince readers of something. **T F**

© 2013 The Critical Thinking Co.™ • www.CriticalThinking.com • 800-458-4849

VII. Understanding Analogies (page 87)

To understand analogies, you learned how to write a sentence about the two words in the analogy **before** you looked at the answer choices.

20. **Tired** and **sleep** go together in the same way as:

Write a sentence that describes how "tired" and "sleep" go together.

_____

_____

  a. **bed** and **rest**.
  b. **night** and **quiet**.
  c. **hungry** and **eat**.
  d. **pencil** and **write**.

Think about how each of these answer choices would fit into the sentence that you wrote.

On a test, you do not always have to **write** a sentence about the two words in an analogy. However, you should always **think** about a sentence that describes how those words go together.

Math Skills for Tests

VIII. Estimate the Correct Answer (page 98)

Whenever you solve a math problem with a lot of digits, you can check your work by estimating the correct answer.

 Below, a student named Derrick is rounding numbers so that he will be able to work with only 1 digit when he estimates the correct answer. **Check Derrick's work, and tell him whether he has rounded numbers correctly or incorrectly.**

21. The number is 762.

<u>7</u>62   First, I underline the place I'm rounding to, which is the 100s place.

<u>7</u>62   The 2 is less than 5, so the underlined number stays the same. The round number is <u>700</u>.

Correct or incorrect? _____   If incorrect, what should the answer be? _____

22. The number is 981.

<u>9</u>81   First, I underline the place I'm rounding to, which is the 100s place.

<u>9</u>81   The 8 is one place to the right.
8 is more than 5, so the underlined number goes up one.
That means that the 9 changes to a 10. The round number is <u>1,000</u>.

Correct or incorrect? _____   If incorrect, what should the answer be? _____

Below is what Derrick says about rounding numbers. Decide if he is correct or incorrect.

23. The number is 529.

Usually, you should round numbers so that you have only 1 digit to work with. So, if I have the number 529, I can round it to 500.

Correct or incorrect? _____

24. What is a more accurate (closer to the real answer) way to round numbers?

If you want to estimate in a way that is more accurate, you can round numbers so that you work with 2 digits.

So, if I have the number 529, and I want a more accurate estimate, I can round 529 to 530.

Correct or incorrect? _____

© 2013 The Critical Thinking Co.™ • www.CriticalThinking.com • 800-458-4849

IX. Solve Complicated Word Problems (page 105),
X. Different Units of Measure (page 133), and XI. Estimation (page 155)

Many students think that word problems can be confusing. You learned four steps that can help you make word problems less confusing and easier to solve.

Below are 4 steps that can help you to solve complicated word problems. **Try to remember these steps, because you will be asked about them on the next page.**

Step 1: Underline the question.

As you read the problem, underline the question that you will need to answer.

Step 2: List the facts (label each number).

Then list the facts (label each number) that you will need in order to find the answer. The facts are numbers and information you need to solve the problem.

Step 3: Write a math sentence. Label your answer.

Use the numbers in your list to write a math sentence. Sometimes, you will need to write more than one math sentence.

Step 4: Check your answer.

Look at the part of the word problem that you underlined. Does your answer make sense?

25. Below are the steps that you reviewed above. Write the important words that are missing in the blank spaces.
   a. Step 1: As you read the problem, _____ the question that you will need to answer.
   b. Step 2: Then _____ the facts that you will need in order to find the answer.
   c. Step 3: Write a _____ _____. (Sometimes you will write more than one.)
   d. Step 4: Check your _____.

26. True or False: Word problems can sometimes have numbers and information that you <u>do not</u> need in order to solve the problem. _____

27. Let's say that you are having trouble <u>writing math sentences</u>. What can you do to help yourself?
   a. Make sure to write labels on the numbers in the math sentences, and also write labels on the answer to each math sentence.
   b. Draw pictures; then write labels on the pictures.
   c. Think about key words that tell you what operation to use (+, -, x, or ÷).
   d. all of the above

© 2013 The Critical Thinking Co.™ • www.CriticalThinking.com • 800-458-4849

28. What do you do when you <u>check your answer</u>?

    a. Think about the people and animals in the word problem. Make sure that they are all represented in your answer.

    b. Check all the other word problems that you are asked to solve. Make sure that your solutions are all the same.

    c. Look at the first sentence of the word problem. Make sure that it makes sense.

    d. Look at the part of the word problem that you underlined in Step 1. Make sure that you answered the right question.

29. Cassidy is solving the following word problem. Her work appears below the problem.

Milo is a baby giraffe at a zoo. He is growing and eats a lot. On Monday, he ate 11 pounds of leaves. On Tuesday, he ate 12 pounds of leaves. On Wednesday, he ate another 12 pounds of leaves. <u>How many pounds of leaves did Milo eat on Monday, Tuesday, and Wednesday</u>? ←2

$$
\begin{array}{ll}
\text{11 pounds} & \quad 11 \\
\text{12 pounds} & +\ 12 \\
\text{12 pounds} & \underline{+\ 12} \\
\uparrow 1 & \quad \text{35 pounds of leaves eaten on Mon., Tues., and Wed.} \leftarrow 3
\end{array}
$$

There are numbers next to parts of Cassidy's work. Each of the numbers matches one of the steps that you've learned. Write the number that matches the steps that Cassidy used to solve the problem.

    a. Underline the question you need to answer. _____

    b. List (label) the facts you'll need to solve the problem. _____

    c. Write a math sentence and check your answer. _____

30. Omar is taking a test. On the test, he solves the same word problem that Cassidy solved. His work is shown below:

Milo is a baby giraffe at a zoo. He is growing and eats a lot. On Monday, he ate 11 pounds of leaves. On Tuesday, he ate 12 pounds of leaves. On Wednesday, he ate another 12 pounds of leaves. <u>How many pounds of leaves did Milo eat on Monday, Tuesday, and Wednesday</u>?

$$11 + 11 + 12 = 35$$

Even though it does not show in his work, Omar *thought* about the steps he learned as he solved the word problem.

Is it okay that Omar wrote a number sentence without writing the facts and labeling his answer?

    a. No! The facts must be written out every time in order to make sure you are thinking carefully.

    b. Yes! Omar was thoughtful about the word problem. On a test, you don't always need to write out all the facts, but it *always* helps to *think* about them.

31. Sabrina is solving the word problem below.

Mr. Rogers had a bookcase that was 2 meters high. He added a shelf on top of the bookcase to make it taller. The shelf he added was 80 centimeters tall. After adding the shelf, how tall is Mr. Rogers' bookcase? (hint: 1 meter = 100 centimeters)

Facts	Facts With Same Unit of Measure
2 meters	_____
80 centimeters	_____

Sabrina needs to change the numbers that she has listed to the same unit of measure before she writes a math sentence.

Go ahead and change the units of measurements for her. Write the numbers on the lines.

Write the math sentence that Sabrina should use to find the answer.

32. Dylan is solving the word problem below.

Ms. Post hosts a lot of fancy parties. In May, she had a party for 23 guests. In June, she had a party for 29 guests. In July, she had her biggest party, and there were 54 guests. *About* how many guests in all did Ms. Post have at all three of her parties?

Facts	Facts With Rounded Numbers
23 guests	_____
29 guests	_____
54 guests	_____

Dylan should round the numbers that she has listed before she writes a math sentence.

Go ahead and change the facts to facts with rounded numbers. Write the numbers on the lines.

Write the math sentence that Dylan should use to find the answer.

© 2013 The Critical Thinking Co.™ • www.CriticalThinking.com • 800-458-4849

XII. Understand Charts (page 173)

A chart can tell you a lot of information very quickly. You learned some things about charts that you will be asked about in the questions below.

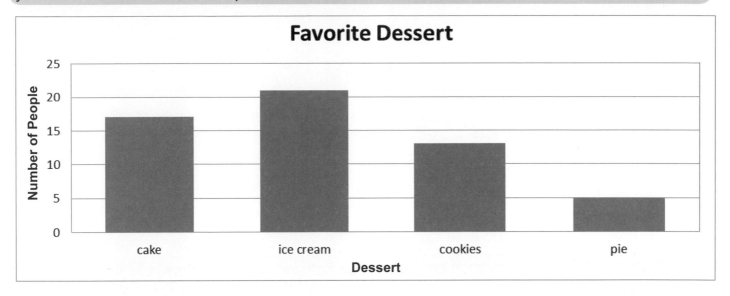

33. Luke looks at the bar graph above and says, "Only one person said that pie was his favorite dessert!" Luke has made a mistake. He made a mistake because he did not look carefully at the chart's:

      a. scale.
      b. title.
      c. labels.

34. Luke has learned from his last mistake. He now knows that 5 people said that pie was their favorite dessert.

However, he makes another mistake. Luke looks at the chart above and says, "There is no way to know how many people say that cake is their favorite dessert because the bar for cake does not stop at a line."

Is Luke correct? What should he do in order to find out how many people say that cake is their favorite dessert?

_____

_____

_____

XIII. Understand Patterns (page 184)

Sometimes on a test, you will see a series of numbers, or a set of pictures, and you will be asked, "What comes next?"

In order to figure out what comes next in a pattern, you learned that all patterns follow a rule. You leaned the types of rules (increasing, decreasing, or repeating) and that some patterns follow more than one rule.

35. Jessie looks at the math pattern below and says, "I know that the pattern is increasing, because the numbers keep going up. But I still don't know what number comes next!"

2, 3, 5, 8, 12, 17, ?

What should Jessie do now in order to figure out what number comes next?
    a. Figure out if the pattern is also repeating.
    b. Figure out if the pattern is also decreasing.
    c. Do some math in order to figure out more about the rule of the pattern. She should figure out how much the numbers increase each time.
    d. Take a guess.

36. Jessie tries to figure out more about the pattern. Her work is shown below. Circle the letter of the work that will help her figure out the correct answer.

a.
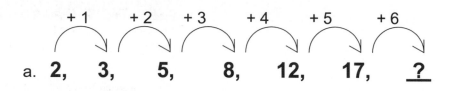

b.
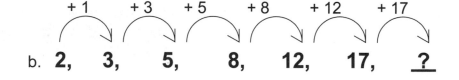

c.

+ 1   + 2   + 3   + 3   + 2   + 1

2,   3,   5,   8,   12,   17,   ?

© 2013 The Critical Thinking Co.™ • www.CriticalThinking.com • 800-458-4849

Answer Key

If some of your answers are wrong, that's normal. Good students do not always answer each question correctly, but they try to figure out why their answer is incorrect. If you answer a question incorrectly but then try again to figure out the right answer, you should be proud of yourself. Trying again is what makes you successful!

I. Vocabulary (pp. 1-14)

1. no, yes, no, no; b

2. no, no, yes, no; c

3. yes, no, yes, no; a. "c. beautiful" makes sense, but "a. great" is the best answer.

4. yes, no, no, no; a

5. c; "Poisonous" makes the most sense. Even though the frogs look harmless, they are actually poisonous.

6. a; "Made" makes the most sense. "d. washed" does not make sense at all. "b. found" and "c. bought" are not the best answers.

7. d; "Responsible" is the only choice that makes sense.

8. c; All of the other answer choices make sense, but "c. built" is the best answer.

9. b; "a. very dirty" makes sense, but "b. very happy" is the best answer. "Exuberant" means "very happy."

10. a; "Fear" makes the most sense. Some kids might choose "b. practice," because you have to practice in order to learn how to swim. However, "practice" is not the best answer.

11. b; "Gather" is the answer that makes the most sense. Some kids might choose "a. read" because book clubs read books. But the word "read" does not make sense in the sentence.

12. d; "Country" is the best answer. Some kids might choose "a. fun" because carnivals are fun, but the word "fun" does not make sense in the sentence.

13. a; "b. funny" makes sense, but "a. hurried" is the answer. "Hasty" means "hurried" or "quick."

14. b; "Golden" is the only answer that makes sense in the sentence.

15. b; "Zoo" is the only answer that makes sense. You might see animals in the country, in the mountains, and at a pet store, but you probably will not see monkeys and elephants in those places. You probably will see monkeys and elephants in a zoo.

16. b; "Leaped" is the best answer because the acrobat must leap in order to land on his partner's shoulders.

17. a; "Delicious" is the only answer that makes sense in the sentence.

18. b; "Enormous" is the only answer that makes sense in the sentence.

19. d; "a. cloth" makes sense, but "d. strong" is the best answer.

20. d; "c. neglectful" makes sense, but "d. interested" is the best answer.

21. c; "a. heat up" and "b. melt" might seem to make sense, but actually, you cannot see a gold dome heat up or melt. However, you can see a gold dome flash. "Glint" means "flash."

22. d; All of the other answer choices make sense, however, "antique" means "very old."

23. c; "d. athletic" makes sense, but "c. determined" is the answer. "Dogged" means "determined."

24. a; "Withheld" is the only answer that makes sense in the sentence.

25. d; "a. ocean" and "c. zoo" make sense, but "d. aquarium" is the best answer.

26. a; "b. problem" makes sense, but "a. disaster" is the best answer.

II. Understand the Main Idea (pp. 15-28)

1. Any answer that describes animals and plants that live in the ocean is correct.

2. Any answer that describes writing or communicating is correct.

3. Any answer that describes fruit or things to eat is correct.

4. Any answer that describes animals or pets is correct.

7. Any paragraph that states the main idea and then goes on to describe some details is correct.
   For example:
   > I like eating fruits. There are a lot of fruits you can eat. Some people like bananas and apples. Some people even eat a fruit called a kiwi fruit. My favorite is watermelon.

8. Any paragraph that states the main idea and then goes on to describe some details is correct.
   For example:
   > Animals can be kept as pets. Fish, turtles, dogs, and cats all make good pets. I would love to have a rabbit as a pet.

9. a

10. a

11. c

12. b

13. a

14. d

15. Any title that describes a noisy library is correct.
    For example:
    > The Noisy Library
    > A Library Is NOT Always Quiet

16. Any title about ending violin lessons and taking guitar lessons instead is correct.
    For example:
    > Why I Want to Stop Violin Lessons and Start Guitar Lessons
    > Trading Guitar Lessons for Violin Lessons

17. Main idea of the first paragraph: Early in White House history, most pets were farm animals. Main idea of the second paragraph: In more recent years, White House pets have been cats and dogs. Main idea of the whole passage: a

18. Main idea of first paragraph: Telescopes used by scientists are very powerful.
    Main idea of second paragraph: Telescopes used by people who are not scientists are not as powerful. Main idea of the whole passage: b

19. b

20. a; This is a tough choice between "a" and "c." Of the two choices, "a" is the best answer because the main idea is not just that wild horses are smaller than domestic horses, but also that their short legs are a good thing.

21. Any title about eyelids is correct. The title must be about eyelids, and not just eyes.

22. Main idea of the first paragraph: Becky felt cheerful because it was a bright fall day. Main idea of the second paragraph: Becky became discouraged because she had to rake the fall leaves. Main idea of the whole passage: a

III. Multiple Choice Questions (pp. 29-40)

1. b

2. c

3. a

4. a; The main idea is not just about polar bears, but about polar bears' fur and skin. Even when the passage talks about cute polar bear cubs, it goes on to say that they are cute because of their cuddly white fur. Also, when polar bears hunt, their white fur helps them to hide in the snow.

5. a

6. c

7. d

8. b

9. a

10. c; Even though "b" is also correct, "c" is the best answer.

11. d

12. c

13. d; Look at the three headings of the passage. The three headings give a clue about the main idea of each of the three sections of the passage.

14. a

15. b

16. c

17. a

18. b; The first paragraph states that the soles of your feet have more nerve endings than your ankles, and that's why the soles of your feet are more ticklish than your ankles.

19. c; You cannot tickle yourself because you cannot surprise yourself with your own movements. Choice "d" sounds impressive, because it has a big word in it, "cerebellum," but it actually is incorrect. Your cerebellum does not help you pay attention to movements that are made by other people and things.

20. b

© 2013 The Critical Thinking Co.™ • www.CriticalThinking.com • 800-458-4849

V. Use Clues to Infer Answers (pp. 58-70)

If you were incorrect in answering questions 3-8, make sure you **re-read the clues** that are given after every question. When you re-read the clues, you might understand the question, and the answer, in a different way.

3. a; This is a tough choice between "a" and "d." Choice "a" is the best answer. Giving up his birthday wish to someone else would have been a kind thing to do, but his mother wanted Kwan to have his birthday wish for himself.

4. b

5. c

6. d

7. d

8. a; This is a tough choice between "a" and "d." Choice "d" is not correct because Ms. Fermi called the custodian to dispose of the flowers before Laura sat very still with her hand over her mouth. Laura already knew that Ms. Fermi would not touch the flowers and be poisoned, so she must have been worrying about herself.

9. b

10. "The red lizard frowned upon the yellow lizard and said, 'I am too grand a lizard to eat such tiny flies.' "

11. a

12. "He muttered to himself, 'I was too picky.' " The lizard understands that he was too picky. If he learns from his mistake, then the next time that he climbs the high rock, he will eat whatever flies come his way.

13. c; Were the steps used to figure out what the word "gusto" meant? Even if the right answer was chosen, the STEPS should have been used.

14. a

15. The last four lines of the poem can help to figure out the answer to question 14 because they are about someone remembering a block city.

16. Ms. Hernandez is most likely Jasmine's teacher. Even though the question asks for two specific clues from the passage that lead to the answer, there are three specific clues that could have been discussed:
   1. Ms. Hernandez told the class to choose a topic, which is what a teacher would have done.
   2. Ms. Hernandez checked the students' index cards, which is what a teacher would have done.
   3. Ms. Hernandez nodded to give Jasmine encouragement during her presentation, which is what a teacher would have done.

17. d; Even though all the answer choices were lessons that Jasmine learned from having given her shark presentation, the most important lesson, and the best answer, was that Jasmine learned that confidence comes when you do something difficult.

18. c; The other three answer choices were facts that Jasmine said she learned while she was doing research for her presentation.

19. b

20. c; Jasmine said that she thought that this part of the project was great because she loved looking for images on the internet. Even though she learned a lot from presenting the project in front of the class, she did not think that presenting was fun.

21. There were at least two sentences that could have given clues to the answer to question 20. One sentence was, "I thought this part of the project was great, because I love looking for images on the Internet." The other was, "Although presenting the project in front of the class was not fun, I learned a lot from doing something that was very difficult for me."

22. c

23. The next time that Jasmine gives a class presentation, she will probably feel less nervous and more confident because she learned a lot from having given the shark presentation. When she gave the shark presentation, even though she was very nervous, she was able to continue. When she finished, she had a feeling of confidence about what she had done.

24. a

25. c

26. d

VI. Use Your Thoughts and Feelings to Infer Answers (pp. 71-86)

1. b
2. a
3. c
4. a
5. b
6. c
7. Some words that describe the tone of this passage are: "angry," "sad," "upset." Different words are also okay.
8. Some words that describe the tone of this passage are: "nervous," "scared," "frightened." Different words are also okay.
9. Some words that describe the tone of this passage are: "mystical," "peaceful," "sleepy." Different words are also okay.
10. Some words that describe the tone of this passage are: "silly," "weird," "goofy." Different words are also okay.
11. d
12. a
13. A. fact   B. opinion   C. fact   D. opinion   E. opinion   F. opinion   G. fact
14. There are many words used to write a simile. Some examples of words that students used were "quick as a fox" and "fast as a racehorse."
15. a; Some students may be tempted to choose "b," but "b" is a simile.
16. There are many idioms that could have been written!
17. d
18. b
19. b
20. c
21. d
22. b

VII. Understanding Analogies (pp. 87-97)

1. b
2. b
3. d
4. b
5. d
6. d
7. c

8. c
9. b
10. c
11. a
12. a; A square is a type of shape. A banana is a type of fruit.
13. c; A fish lives in a fish tank. A cow lives in a barn.
14. c; A dollar bill is made out of paper. A car is made out of metal.
15. c; A racquet is used to play tennis. A bat is used to play baseball.
16. d; A frog is a type of amphibian. A dog is a type of mammal.
17. c; You can run on a track. You can play on a playground.
18. c; A poodle is a type of dog. Chocolate is a type of flavor.
19. b; Ice feels cold. A pillow feels soft.
20. d; You can eat an apple. You can drink water.
21. b; Always is the opposite of never. All is the opposite of none.
22. a; You can predict things that will happen in the future. You can remember things that happened in the past.
23. a; Weight is measured by a scale. Length is measured by a ruler.
24. c; A doctor is a person who works in a hospital. A teacher is a person who works in a school.
25. c; A baby moves by crawling. A fish moves by swimming.
26. d; Fake is the opposite of real. False is the opposite of true.
27. b; Rain falls in a drop. Snow falls in a flake.
28. c; A square has four sides. A pentagon has five sides.
29. c; Number two is the second place finish. Number one is the winner.
30. b; The opposite of "can" is "can't." There are two choices that are the opposite of "will," "will not" and "won't." "Won't" is the best answer because "won't" is a contraction just as "can't" is a contraction.

© 2013 The Critical Thinking Co.™ • www.CriticalThinking.com • 800-458-4849

VIII. Estimate the Correct Answer
(pp. 98-104)

1. b; The number 15 is not a digit. A digit is a single number between 0-9. The number 15 has two digits, a "1" and a "5."
2. c; 4
3. a; 540,098
4. a; 7
5. b; 2
6. b; hundreds place
7. c. 59
8. c. 97
9. a. 36
10. c. 64
11. d. 30
12. b. 21
13. d. 220
14. c. 6,069
15. b. 262
16. b. 3,463

XII. Understand Charts (pp. 173-183)

1. a
2. b; The bar for green eyes is a little bit above the number 4. 5 is the best estimate.
3. Visitors at the Museum
4. Number of Visitors; Month
5. c
6. a
7. a
8. b
9. b
10. b; Counting the number of tickets that each friend has is easy. Jared has 5 tickets, so he has the most tickets. Luke has 4, and Alicia has 3.
11. a; Figuring out the number of points that each friend has is harder. Math sentences have to be written in order to know how many points each friend has.

    Luke has 2 red tickets worth 10 points each and 2 yellow tickets worth two points each.
    $$2 \times 10 = 20$$
    $$2 \times 2 = 4$$
    20 + 4 = <u>24 points for Luke</u> or <u>Luke has the most points</u>

Jared has 3 blue tickets worth 5 points each and 2 yellow tickets worth two points each.
$$3 \times 5 = 15$$
$$2 \times 2 = 4$$
15 + 4 = <u>19 points for Jared</u>

Alicia has 1 red tickets worth 10 points and 2 blue tickets worth 5 points each.
$$1 \times 10 = 10$$
$$2 \times 5 = 10$$
10 + 10 = <u>20 points for Alicia</u>

12. c; Choices "a" and "b" do not make sense. Choice "d" says, "Which class <u>correctly</u> counted the number of tulips they saw?" We don't know if the classes counted correctly or not. All we know is the number of tulips that each class counted. We can see the class that counted the most tulips. That's why "c" is correct.
13. d; The scale is important. Each picture of a tulip is worth 2 tulips. One half of a tulip is worth 1 tulip.
14. d
15. a
16. d; The bar graph shows that neither the horse nor the dog received the fewest votes for all the kids combined. So "horse" and "dog" should be crossed out. Math sentences have to be written in order to figure out whether the cat or the hamster received the fewest votes from the younger and older kids combined.

    A cat was chosen by about 14 younger kids and 5 older kids.
    14 + 5 = 19. About 19 kids combined chose a cat.

    A hamster was chosen by about 9 younger kids and 7 older kids.
    9 + 7 = 16. About 16 kids combined chose a hamster.

    The hamster received the fewest votes from the younger and older kids combined.
17. d; Choices "a," "b," and "c," should be crossed out because they are wrong. That leaves choice "d." The bar graph shows that about 15 older kids chose a dog, and about 7 chose a hamster. 15 is about twice as much as 7, so "d" is the best choice.

© 2013 The Critical Thinking Co.™ • www.CriticalThinking.com • 800-458-4849

18. a; The survey asks kids about what pet they would choose to take care of for a day. It does not ask if they are scared of any pets or if they own any pets. That's why "b" and "c" are wrong. Choice "d" is wrong because younger kids clearly prefer to take care of a dog more than any other pet, and older kids prefer to take care of a horse.

19. a; The scale says that the population is in thousands. In 1985, the red line for Apple Valley is in between 6,000 and 7,000. 6,500 is the best estimate.

20. There are a lot of different ways to answer this question. The most important things to include are:
   • that Best Apple Pie <u>did</u> seem to change the populations of Apple Valley and Sugar Hill.
   • after Best Apple Pie moved to Apple Valley in 1980, the line graph shows that the population of Apple Valley grew a lot. However, the population of Sugar Hill went down after 1980.

21. b; In order to understand the pie chart, percentages must have been learned in school. "c" might have been chosen because it seems the number of people who chose strawberry ice cream can be figured out. However, it is just a percentage; the numbers are not known.

22. c; 100 people were surveyed, so all the percentages are exactly the same as the number of people. 15% of people said that strawberry was their favorite ice cream flavor, so 15 people said that strawberry was their favorite ice cream flavor. That's why "c" is correct. Choices "a" and "b" are both true, because there were 100 people surveyed. Choice "d" does not make sense at all.

XIII. Understand Patterns (pp. 184-198)

1. The dog comes next.
2. 16
3. 1 orange
4. 2
5. The biggest dog comes next.
6. The black number "11" comes next.
7. d
8. 33

9. a
10. 8
11. b
12. a
13. 3
14. c
15. The pattern is decreasing.
16. Subtract one line each time.
17. 9
18.
19. b
20. Add two (or two more dots) each time.
21. Lionel's performance is getting better, like an increasing pattern. He scores 4 more goals each day.
22. Lionel's performance is staying the same, like a repeating pattern. He is not scoring any more or any fewer goals.
23. Either of the following answers is correct:
   • If Lionel practiced on Sunday, he would probably get in 14 goals, just as he had the previous three days (like a repeating pattern).
   • If Lionel practiced on Sunday, he would improve and get more than 14 goals. He had been improving on Monday through Thursday, so he might start improving again (like an increasing pattern).
24. b; This is three different patterns. The numbers at the top of the boxes increase by one each time the happy faces repeat between white and black, and the color of the boxes also repeat. When at least two of the patterns are figured out, the answer can be figured out.
25. ⬤⬤
      ⬤
26. The pattern decreases. If you look at the red balls in the bottom row, you can see that the bottom row disappears each time.
27. 14
28. a
29. e; This is a very simple repeating pattern: pizza every Friday.
30. c; This also is a repeating pattern. Look at what was served on Wednesday, first, it was Make Your Own Salad. Then, it was Macaroni and Cheese, followed by Tacos, and finally, Chicken Nuggets. The pattern is

© 2013 The Critical Thinking Co.™ • www.CriticalThinking.com • 800-458-4849